dynamic quilts
with easy curves

19 projects to stack, shuffle, and sew

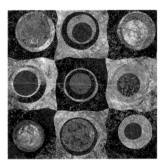

Karla Alexander

Martingale®
& COMPANY

DEDICATION

To quilters everywhere, from whom I've learned so much. You continue to impress and inspire me, fearlessly trying new techniques. You come along for the ride with an open mind and rarely sour at the thought of removing stitches. You sew late into the night, practice my "eye cleansing" and "10-foot rule" with or without laughing, and you entertain and practice my "What would Grandma do (WWGD)?" concept. Thank you! Quilt on and enjoy!

ACKNOWLEDGMENTS

It takes a team to put a book together; no one person does it all. I've enjoyed the help and support of many, from family and friends to the awesome staff at Martingale & Company. Thank you.

I would also like to thank the following for contributing fabric, opportunities, and support:

Westminster Fibers

Greenbaum's Quilted Forest, Salem, Oregon
Fabric Depot, Portland, Oregon

My long-arm quilting wizard, Loretta Orsborn

Rob Krieger, the owner of Checker Distributors, whose encouragement—and willingness to work with me—resulted in a series of rulers that make it possible for everyone to cut and sew curves. I owe him a huge thank-you for adding me to the Creative Grids team of incredible designers, and for believing in me.
Thank you, Rob!

Dynamic Quilts with Easy Curves: 19 Projects to Stack, Shuffle, and Sew
© 2012 by Karla Alexander

That Patchwork Place® is an imprint of Martingale & Company®.

Martingale & Company
19021 120th Ave. NE, Suite 102
Bothell, WA 98011
www.martingale-pub.com

Printed in China
17 16 15 14 13 12   8 7 6 5 4 3 2 1

Library of Congress Cataloging-in-Publication Data is available upon request.

ISBN: 978-1-60468-082-9

Credits

President & CEO: Tom Wierzbicki
Editorial Director: Mary V. Green
Design Director: Paula Schlosser
Managing Editor: Karen Costello Soltys
Technical Editor: Laurie Baker
Copy Editor: Melissa Bryan
Production Manager: Regina Girard
Cover & Text Designer: Shelly Garrison
Illustrator: Laurel Strand
Photographer: Brent Kane

Mission Statement

Dedicated to providing quality products and service to inspire creativity.

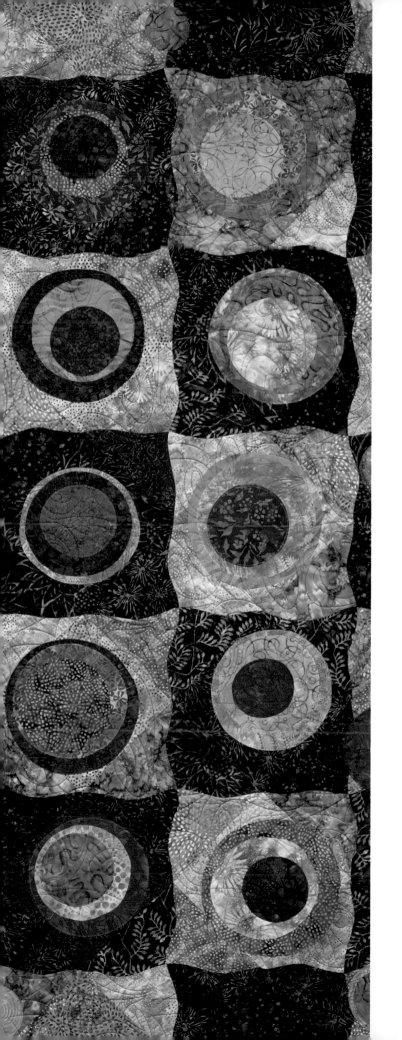

contents

INTRODUCTION 5

QUILTMAKING BASICS 6

STACKING THE DECK 9

FINISHING THE QUILT 13

QUILT PROJECTS

Wild Heart 16

Black of Diamonds 20

Cartwheels 24

First Dawn 28

Penny Lane 32

BIV 36

Diamondback 40

Wavelength 44

Bounce 48

Pisa 52

Village News 56

Split Seconds 60

Watermelon Dreams 64

Epicenter 68

Garden Party 72

Good Vibrations 78

Swish 82

Well Connected 87

Urban Sprawl 92

ABOUT THE AUTHOR 96

introduction

Quilting is a craft that dates back many centuries. Of course, the emphasis in the early days was on providing warmth and protection. Today, quiltmaking not only fulfills those basic needs, but it has evolved into a creative activity enjoyed by men, women, and children of all ages. Modern tools and endless choices of fabric color and design make the *making* of a quilt a lot of fun. In the evolution of quiltmaking, I believe we are living in an excellent time to explore and experiment.

In that spirit of experimentation, I've been playing for a while now with techniques for cutting free-form curves with my "stack the deck" method. I was so happy with the results that I began teaching the technique to my students. Many enjoyed the process; however, it seemed that just as many were uncomfortable with it and preferred a more predetermined outcome. In my attempt to reach the latter group, I designed several specialty rulers for Creative Grids USA, the manufacturer of non-slip rulers. I designed the quilts in this book using these rulers, and while they aren't mandatory, they do make the process easier if you happen to struggle with cutting free-form curves. If you're fearless with your rotary cutter, the designs are just as easy to create following the suggestions with each project. Make your projects as precise or as free-form as you want them to be.

In the following pages, you'll find information for many different techniques, as well as design ideas. The projects in this book are meant to be used as inspiration for your own work. Follow the fabric requirements word by word, or switch things up and make the quilts uniquely your own with completely different colors and block arrangements. Work confidently, using your instincts as you go. If you don't like a particular color or block arrangement, change it until you do—don't settle. The curves are all optional; each and every curve can be replaced with a straight cut. I like to build my quilts one block at a time and I encourage you to do the same.

quiltmaking basics

To make good-quality quilts, you need to use good-quality ingredients and reliable tools. Start with a sewing machine in proper working order, mix in high-quality fabrics and threads, add a generous amount of accuracy, and you'll end up with a successful quilting experience. The following is a rundown of the basic tools and techniques you'll need to make any of the quilts in this book. Refer to this section as necessary when you're making your quilt project.

TOOLS AND SUPPLIES

Before beginning any of the quilting projects, collect the tools and materials required. Purchase the best tools you can afford. Good tools yield good results and make the process more enjoyable.

Rotary-cutting supplies. You'll need a rotary-cutting mat, rotary cutter, and acrylic rulers. My favorite size of cutting mat is 24" x 36"; however, if your space is limited, an 18" x 24" mat will work fine.

In my opinion, you can never have too many rulers. However, I do recommend a few basic sizes for the projects in this book. A 6" x 12" ruler works well for cutting free-form curves and a 6" x 24" ruler is great for cutting long strips. Square rulers are essential for cutting squares and trimming up pieced blocks.

You'll be slicing through many layers of fabric, so it's crucial that you begin each project with a sharp new blade for your rotary cutter. I prefer the medium-sized 45 mm rotary cutter, but a large 60 mm rotary cutter is also nice. Choose whichever one feels best to you.

Mounting tape. I tape this on my sewing machine to use as a guide, which is especially helpful when sewing curves. This is a double-sided tape with foam backing that comes on a roll. If you're concerned about any residue the tape might leave on the bed of your sewing machine, place a piece of blue painter's tape down first.

Sewing machine. Be sure your sewing machine is in good working order and sews a reliable and balanced straight stitch. If you plan to machine quilt, you'll need a walking foot and possibly a darning foot, depending on the style of quilting you choose.

Sewing thread. Use good-quality, 100%-cotton thread. I like to use neutral colors for piecing blocks.

Spray sizing. I'm a huge fan of spray sizing. Using it to press my fabrics before cutting or piecing helps fight distortion by keeping the edges of my pieces nice and crisp.

FABRIC CHOICES

Most likely the first thing you think about when making a quilt is color. It's much more enjoyable to work with colors you like than those you don't. I find that over the years my color palette continues to change and expand. Try to keep an open mind when making your fabric selections. Preview several different colors and prints before settling, and once you get started on your project, never be afraid to change your mind! Go with your instincts!

I prefer to work in groups of at least three fabrics for each value in a block. For example, when choosing a print for the light part of a block, I'll preview many different selections. Working in groups of three or more helps distribute colors and prints throughout your quilt so that one particular print or color doesn't stick out. I lay out my choices and then apply my "10-foot rule" along with an "eye cleansing" (both explained on page 7) before making my final choice.

Blocks for these quilts can be made from a wide assortment of colors and prints, just as in any traditionally pieced quilt. They can also be more controlled, with a planned color scheme or theme-related fabric such as holiday or baby. Choose the theme for your quilt, and then start the preview process.

Before beginning any project, I always check my stash to see if there's something I can use. The quilts in this book make it especially easy to toss in an extra replacement square or two, as long as it plays well with what you've already selected. I find adding more fabric to the mix spices thing up! If you look closely at the photographs, you'll probably detect that some of the quilts contain more fabrics than the instructions call for. I challenge you to go through your stash and use what you already own!

The 10-Foot Rule

Whether you're using new fabrics or fabrics from your stash, you'll need to preview each of them before inviting them into your quilt. If you're at the quilt store, stand the bolts of fabric side by side, and then back up approximately 10 feet and take a look. If you're at home working from your stash, fan the fabrics out across your design wall or lay them out across the top of a couch so the fabrics can be viewed vertically. Do the fabrics contrast well with one another? If one fabric appears to jump out from the rest, it may need another companion (or two) for a better balance. Remember to try and work in groups of three.

On the other hand, if you have three fabrics from the same color group, use the 10-foot rule to determine if they appear to blend together too much, resembling a single piece of fabric. Instead of having three medium blues that all muddle together, swap one out for a brighter blue, a blue that has another color in the print, or something to liven up the group.

One of my favorite tools for evaluating fabric and quilt block layouts is a simple door peephole, available at any home-improvement center. Looking through a peephole distances you from your fabric choices and helps determine if you have a "jumper" (a fabric that jumps out from the rest) or if you have too many fabrics that blend together, becoming indistinguishable. The peephole is simply another tool to achieve the same result as my 10-foot rule.

Eye Cleansing

During the fabric-selection process, I also use a technique I call eye cleansing. Once my fabrics are arranged for viewing, I turn and look at anything that is a totally different color for several seconds. For example, if you're picking pastels, turn and look out the window at a bright green lawn or the sky. If you're choosing a warm red and orange palette, turn and let your eyes find something that is dark black or dark brown. Once you've looked at other colors for a few

seconds, turn back and look at your fabric selection. If a fabric doesn't seem to fit or doesn't appear to add anything to the mix, go with your first reaction and pull that fabric out or replace it. Continue using the 10-foot rule or door peephole and the eye cleansing method until you're satisfied with your selections.

FUSIBLE-WEB APPLIQUÉ

"Bounce" (page 48) and "Garden Party" (page 72) include designs created with fusible-web appliqué. Paper-backed fusible web is sold in both heavyweight and lightweight varieties. For this book, I used the lightweight fusible web and added machine stitching over the raw edges of the appliqué shapes. For appliqués that won't be stitched, I recommend that you use a heavier-weight fusible web. Because the fusible web is applied to the wrong side of the fabric, patterns for fusible-web appliqué are given in mirror image.

1. Trace each part of the selected appliqué design onto the paper side of the fusible web. Roughly cut around the traced designs on the fusible web. Don't cut on the traced lines at this point.

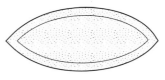

Fusible appliqué shape

2. Position each cut fusible shape, web side down, on the wrong side of the selected fabrics and press, following the manufacturer's instructions for the fusible web. Cut out each shape on the drawn lines. Remove the paper backing.

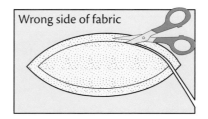

Wrong side of fabric

3. Arrange the shapes in the desired positions on the right side of the background fabric. Use an iron to fuse the shapes in place according to the manufacturer's instructions.

4. Sew around the edges of each appliqué shape using a machine buttonhole stitch, straight stitch, satin stitch, or zigzag stitch.

ASSEMBLING THE QUILT TOP

Once all your blocks are complete, it's time for the layout. Arrange your blocks in rows according to the project instructions (or use you own arrangement). Play with the blocks—twisting, turning, and substituting them—until you're satisfied. I try to separate identical prints so that they don't end up next to each other in the finished quilt. View your arrangements from a distance using my "10-foot rule" (page 7) to check the visual balance.

Join your blocks into rows, matching the seams between the blocks. I like to pin each row to prevent any surprises once I'm done. Press seam allowances in the opposite direction from row to row so that opposing seams butt against each other. Join the rows of blocks into sets of two rows and then sew the sets together.

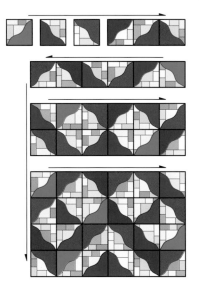

ADDING BORDERS

Most of the quilts in this book have some sort of border. Some are pieced and others rely on plain borders to enhance the blocks. Refer to the project instructions to make pieced borders; follow the steps below for plain borders.

1. Refer to the project's cutting instructions to cut the required number of border strips.

2. Remove the selvages and sew the border strips together end to end to make one long strip. Press seam allowances to one side.

3. Fold the long border strip in half widthwise, matching short ends. Vertically center the folded border directly under the quilt top so there's excess extending at the top and bottom edges. Make sure the border and the quilt top are smooth without any wrinkles or pleats. Trim the doubled border strip even with the edges of the quilt top.

Trim border strip even
with quilt top and bottom.

4. Mark the halfway point of the border length and the sides of the quilt top with a pin. Pin the borders to opposite sides of the quilt, matching center marks and ends. Sew the borders in place, easing in any fullness. Press seam allowances toward the borders.

5. Repeat steps 3 and 4, centering the border strip horizontally under the quilt top, to cut and add the top and bottom borders.

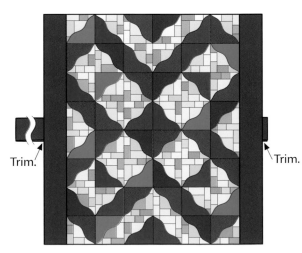

stacking the deck

The projects in this book use my "stack the deck" technique. With this method you stack fabric squares or rectangles right sides up into a "deck" and then slice the deck into various shapes. The order of the fabrics is shuffled and then the pieces are sewn back together. This method gives you the advantage of using many different fabrics without having to mess around with a lot of math. If you want more blocks than the pattern calls for, you can usually start with as many squares or rectangles as you would like completed blocks. This makes it easy to check out your stash and rediscover a few favorite pieces of which you only have a small amount left. As long as you can cut it into a square or rectangle as required in the quilt pattern, you can usually use it. I love that option!

STACKING THE FABRIC DECKS

Once you cut the required number of squares or rectangles, stack the number of pieces indicated in the pattern right side up for rotary cutting. Arrange colors as directed for each individual quilt. Stack the squares or rectangles as neatly as you can, keeping the edges even. Keep in mind that the top fabric will eventually be moved to the bottom of the deck, so it's a good idea to make sure that sufficient contrast exists between the top and bottom fabrics. I like to lay out my deck, fanning the layers on top of one another to make sure I haven't duplicated any fabrics and to make sure I like the mix in the deck. Place a straight pin through all layers in each stack to prevent a mixup.

SLICING THE DECKS

The instructions for each project include a block cutting, shuffling, and sewing guide. Slice your decks apart first, following the order of the C numbers. Cut the line labeled C1, first, followed by C2, and so forth.

Occasionally a project will have you make a few extra blocks in order to keep an equal balance of fabrics

in a deck. The extra blocks give you more choices in the final block layout and can be used on the back of the quilt or in another project. I strongly suggest slicing and sewing one deck at a time. This allows you the opportunity to make desired changes along the way. Use a chalk marker to draw the cutting lines if you'd like. Brush away lines if you don't like them and redraw until you're satisfied.

CUTTING CURVES

When cutting curves, always use a ruler so that you don't lop off a finger or two! Using a ruler also helps keep the fabric nice and flat without any pleats or tucks. I like to use a narrow ruler no longer than 12". I place the ruler on a stack of fabric and gently slide it into a curve as my rotary cutter travels with it. This takes a bit of practice but can be mastered before you know it!

When cutting squares and rectangles in half to make triangles, the first 1" and the last 1" both need to be cut at a perfect 45° angle. This is necessary so that the seam allowances finish nicely into the corner. If you use the Curves for Squares ruler or Curves for Rectangles ruler, the angle is marked for you. If you're cutting the curve free-form, it's a good idea to mark the first and last 1" with a chalk marker, and then draw the curve between the two lines.

SHUFFLING THE DECKS

Shuffling simply means rearranging the fabric segments once they've been cut. By shuffling each stack of fabrics in a specific order, you'll create the correct arrangement of fabrics in each block. Each project in this book has a different shuffling process, which is indicated in the block cutting, shuffling, and sewing guide. To shuffle, follow the S numbers on each piece to move that quantity of pieces from the top of the stack to the

creative grids specialty rulers

I designed the following Creative Grids rulers to be used with many of the designs in this book. While each project can be completed without the rulers, using them offers a bit more stability. To see demonstration videos for each of the rulers, go to www.creativegridsusa.com.

curves for squares ruler (a)

This ruler is used to cut a gentle curve across the diagonal of squares from 5" to 10". Sew the pieces from two different fabrics back together to make squares with a sense of movement. The pieced squares can replace any square unit in a traditional block. Pieced squares finish to approximately 1" less than the cut size.

curves for rectangles ruler (b)

This ruler does for rectangles what the Curves for Squares ruler does for squares. Choose from seven different sizes of rectangles to create a dramatic effect in your finished piece. Pieced rectangles finish to approximately 1" less than the cut size.

straight out of line ruler (c)

The Straight Out of Line ruler creates unique Four Patch blocks with the illusion of curves. Ruler markings make it possible to cut squares from 4" to 10" and every ½" in between. The finished size of the pieced blocks is approximately ¾" less than the cut block.

curved slotted ruler (d)

Cut rectangles into seven curvy shapes to create curvy rail fence units. After the curves are cut from a 9" x 13" rectangle, sew the pieces together and then trim the piece to 8½" square.

split seconds ruler (e)

The Split Seconds ruler helps cut a gentle S curve from squares, rectangles, or pieced blocks from 7" to 18" in length. The finished block size is approximately ¾" less than the cut size. This ruler works with sizes from 7" to 18" in length and can be used with rectangles or squares.

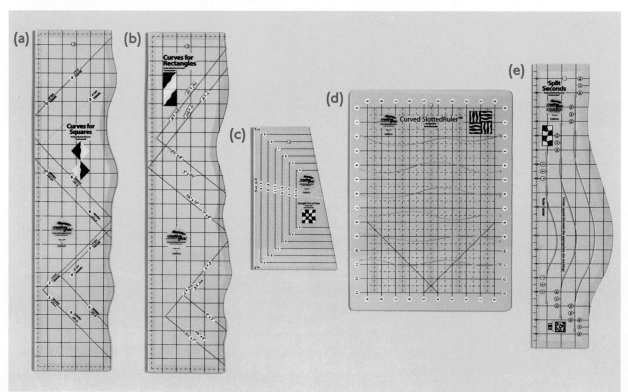

bottom of the stack. For instance, if the piece is labeled S2, you would move the top two pieces from the top of the stack to the bottom of the stack.

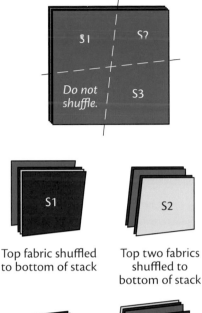

S1

Top fabric shuffled
to bottom of stack

S2

Top two fabrics
shuffled to
bottom of stack

One stack
unshuffled

S3

Top three fabrics
shuffled to
bottom of stack

PREPARING A PAPER LAYOUT

Once you've completed the shuffling process, reassemble the block and pin the stacks for each block to a piece of paper through all layers. Be sure to keep the segments in the exact order and position in which you shuffled them. Once the segments are secure, use a pencil and trace along the cutting lines onto the paper. The pins will help keep the segments in order and the lines will create a template reference.

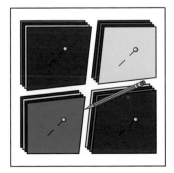

SEWING THE BLOCKS

Sew the blocks as instructed on the block cutting, shuffling, and sewing guide for each project, following the number given in the box on each piece. It's important to keep the segment stacks in their shuffled order while sewing; otherwise you'll end up unintentionally duplicating a fabric within a block. I strongly recommend that you place a safety pin in the top layer of the first segment to be sewed. This way, if you're chain piecing you'll always know which pieces belong to the top layer and that the sewed segments which follow are in the correct sequence.

Sewing Curves

Most of the quilts in this book have blocks or borders that include curves. To maintain accuracy as well as stabilize the fabric pieces, I always use spray sizing to treat pieces that will have curves cut into them. I also mark the center of the curve on both pieces so that the pieces line up correctly when sewn, and I pin the pieces together to keep them aligned while sewing. To prevent pleats, always sew with the needle-down feature engaged on your sewing machine and place mounting tape (see page 6) on the bed of your sewing machine to use as a guide. Apply a 1" to 2" strip of tape ¼" from the needle, extending it in front of the presser foot as shown. Gently align the curved edges of the fabric approximately 1" to 2" in front of the needle and up against the edge of the mounting tape as you sew.

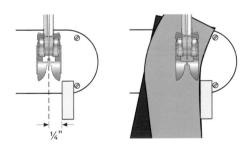

¼"

Chain Piecing

Use chain piecing as indicated in the project instructions. Chain piece by flipping piece 2 onto piece 1 with right sides together and then sewing along the edge. Without breaking the thread, sew pieces 1 and 2 from the next layer together. Continue with each layer, sewing piece 1 to piece 2 without breaking the thread in between.

In some of the projects you can continue to sew segments to the chain-pieced units without cutting the threads between them. After the segments are sewn together, press the seams as indicated, cut the units apart, and restack them in the exact order they were before sewing. Press the seams as necessary. Continue adding segments together in numerical order; then sew together combined units as instructed.

Flippers

A "flipper" results when you attempt to match the seams of two pieces to be sewn together and the seam allowances of both pieces are pressed in the same direction. Seam allowances nest better and lie flatter when the seam allowances are pressed in opposing directions, so when they aren't, you must create a flipper. To do this, flip one of the seam allowances in the opposite direction so they nest together. Sew the seam; then clip the flipped seam allowance ½" from the seam intersection. Clip up to but not through the stitching line. Press the clipped portion flat.

Joining Angled Seams

To create sharp points when joining two segments with angled seams, such as for the blocks in "Epicenter" (page 68) and "Garden Party" (page 72), pin the pieces together first, and then open them up to check the alignment. Often your seams will be offset by ¼" or more.

TRIMMING BLOCKS

In some of the projects, segments will need to be trimmed before they're sewn. This is due to seam allowances; the pieced segments shrink up and are smaller than the unpieced segments to which they'll be added. Trim the excess fabric as instructed to create even edges for the next piece.

Blocks with curves or a lot of seams may end up different sizes or become distorted and "out of square." If this happens, you can often trim the blocks, making the quilt assembly much easier. If size is not critical, trim to the size of your smallest block. Place a square ruler on top of the block and trim two sides. Align the trimmed edges with the correct measurement line on the ruler and trim the remaining two sides.

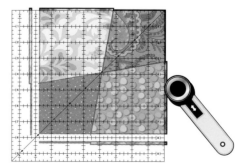

finishing the quilt

Once your quilt top is completed, you'll need to assemble it into a "quilt sandwich," which consists of the backing, batting, and quilt top. The quilt batting and backing should always be at least 4" to 6" larger than the quilt top.

1. Spread the backing wrong side up on a flat surface. Anchor it with pins or masking tape.

2. Spread the batting over the backing, smoothing out any wrinkles.

3. Center the quilt top on the batting.

Basting

For hand quilting, baste with a needle and thread. Start in the center and work diagonally, corner to corner, with large stitches. Next, baste in a grid, stitching horizontal and vertical rows across the quilt top. Space the rows approximately 6" apart. Finish by stitching all around the quilt perimeter.

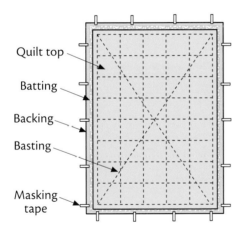

Quilt top

Batting

Backing

Basting

Masking tape

Pin baste if you plan to machine quilt. Pin basting is done most easily if you have a large table for laying out the quilt. Place 1" rustproof safety pins every 5" to 6" across the quilt top, beginning in the center and working your way to the outer edges. Place the pins where they won't interfere with the stitches of your planned quilting design.

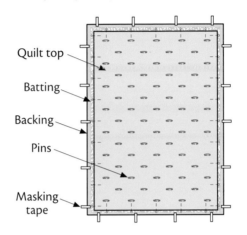

Quilt top

Batting

Backing

Pins

Masking tape

Quilting

Now is the time to give some attention to choosing a quilting design. I make the decision based on several factors. I consider the size of the quilt and whether it's something I can handle, and I also think about the design itself—whether the quilt is intense, simply needing a quilt pattern that won't detract from the design, or whether it would benefit from a fancy quilt pattern. Study your quilt and imagine how you would like the finished product to look. I often quilt small quilts using the "stitch-in-the-ditch" method, in which the quilting lines are stitched into the patch seam lines so that the quilting stitches are practically invisible on the right side of the patchwork. For quilts that are larger and more difficult to manage, I often choose to send them to a professional long-arm quilter.

Binding

Binding finishes the edges of your quilt. I prefer a double-fold, straight-grain binding, often referred to as a French-fold binding. I preview my choices by placing a folded edge under the quilt top, peeking out just enough so that it shows me how the binding would look. If I don't want the binding to stand out too much, I choose a color similar to the border (or, in the event there is no border, similar to the blocks). See "First Dawn" (page 28) for an example. Other times I like to use a totally new color to liven things up a bit, as in the quilt "Village News" (page 56). I very rarely choose the binding ahead of time, preferring to wait until I see how the quilt looks and then previewing my choices at that time. Don't forget to use the "10-foot rule" (page 7) to check out your binding options and see how they look to you.

To make double-fold binding:

1. Trim the batting and backing even with the quilt top.

2. Refer to the cutting list for your project and cut the required number of binding strips.

3. Remove the selvages and place the strips right sides together as shown. Sew the strips together with diagonal seams to make one long binding strip. Trim the excess fabric, leaving a ¼" seam allowance, and press the seam allowances open to reduce bulk.

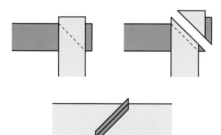

4. Fold the strip in half lengthwise, wrong sides together, and press.

5. I always use my walking foot when attaching binding. Beginning about 18" from a corner, place the binding right sides together with the quilt top. Align the raw edges. Leave a 10" tail and use a ¼" seam allowance to sew the binding to the front of your quilt. Stop sewing ¼" from the first corner and carefully backstitch two or three stitches. Clip the thread and remove the quilt from the machine.

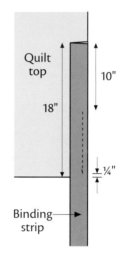

6. Rotate the quilt 90° so that you can work on the next side. Fold the binding up, creating a 45° angle, and then back down, even with the second side of the quilt. A little pleat will form at the corner.

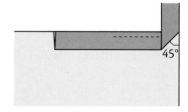

7. Resume stitching at the folded edge of the binding as shown. Continue stitching the binding to the quilt, turning the corners as described, until you're approximately 10" from the point at which you started sewing the binding. Remove the quilt from the sewing machine.

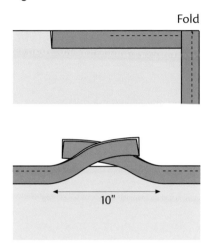

Fold

10"

8. Fold back the beginning and ending tails of the binding strips so that they meet in the center of the unsewn portion of the quilt edge. Finger-press the folded edges.

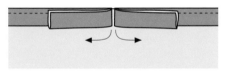

9. Unfold both ends of the binding and match the center points of the two finger-pressed folds, forming an X as shown. Pin and sew the two ends together on the diagonal of the fold lines. Trim the excess binding ¼" from the seam. Finger-press the new seam allowances open and refold the binding. Finish sewing the binding to the quilt.

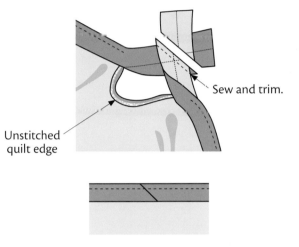

Sew and trim.

Unstitched quilt edge

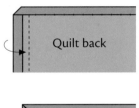

10. Fold the binding over the edge of the quilt top to the back of the quilt, making sure to cover the machine stitching. Hand sew the binding in place, mitering the corners as you go.

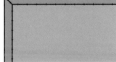

Quilt back

wild heart

Who doesn't love hearts?! They're universal; we can all identify with the sweetness of a heart. This quilt is dedicated to my friend Melanie, born on Valentine's Day.

Finished Quilt: 56½" x 70"

Finished Heart Block: 6½" x 7½"

Finished Pieced Border Block: 7½" x 8½"

Blocks Needed: 42 Heart and 28 Border

fabric tips

Choose a mix of your favorite colors in groups of lights and darks. The main goal is sharp contrast so the hearts "pop" from the background. The background fabric trades places with each block, appearing as the heart in one and the background in another.

MATERIALS

⅜ yard *each* of 6 assorted red prints for blocks

⅜ yard *each* of 6 assorted white-with-black prints for blocks

⅓ yard *each* of 5 assorted red and/or black prints for pieced outer border

⅓ yard *each* of 5 assorted white-with-black prints for pieced outer border

¼ yard of black print for inner border

⅝ yard of fabric for binding

4 yards of fabric for backing

63" x 76" piece of batting

CUTTING

From *each* of the 6 red and 6 white-with-black prints for blocks, cut:

1 strip, 11" x 42"; crosscut into 4 rectangles, 9½" x 11" (48 total; you'll have 6 rectangles left over)

From *each* of the 5 red or black and 5 white-with-black prints for pieced outer border, cut:

1 strip, 9¾" x 42"; crosscut into 3 rectangles, 9¾" x 13" (30 total; you'll have 2 rectangles left over)

From the black print for inner border, cut:

5 strips, 1½" x 42"

From the fabric for binding, cut:

7 strips, 2½" x 42"

MAKING THE HEART BLOCKS

Refer to "Stacking the Deck" on pages 9–12 for details as needed.

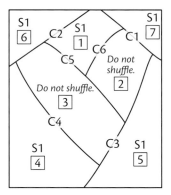

Heart Block Cutting, Shuffling, and Sewing Guide
C = Cutting order
S = Shuffling order
☐ = Sewing order
Cut size: 9½" x 11"

1. Arrange the 9½" x 11" rectangles into 21 decks with one red rectangle and one white-with-black rectangle in each deck.

2. Refer to the block cutting, shuffling, and sewing guide on page 16 to cut each deck. Cut each deck slightly different from one to the next. Draw lines on the top rectangle of each deck to mark the cutting lines, if needed.

3. Shuffle each deck as indicated on the block cutting, shuffling, and sewing guide. Secure each shuffled deck to a piece of paper with a pin through all layers until you're ready to sew.

4. Referring to "Sewing Curves" on page 11, sew the shuffled segments together to make two blocks from each deck for a total of 42 blocks. Trim the blocks to 7" x 8".

MAKING THE BORDER BLOCKS

Refer to "Stacking the Deck" on pages 9–12 for details as needed.

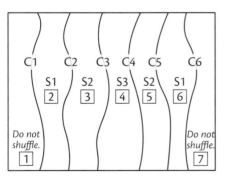

Border Block Cutting, Shuffling, and Sewing Guide
C = Cutting order
S = Shuffling order
▢ = Sewing order
Cut size: 9¾" x 13"

1. Arrange the 9¾" x 13" rectangles into two decks with three red or black rectangles and three white-with-black rectangles in each deck, and four decks with two red or black rectangles and two

white-with-black rectangles in each deck. Alternate the red and black rectangles with the white-with-black rectangles in each deck.

2. Refer to the block cutting, shuffling, and sewing guide below left to cut each deck using the Creative Grids Curved Slotted ruler, or cut the curves free-form by following the instructions in "Cutting Curves" on page 9.

3. Shuffle each deck as indicated on the block cutting, shuffling, and sewing guide. Secure each shuffled deck to a piece of paper with a pin through all layers until ready to sew.

4. Refer to "Sewing Curves" to sew the shuffled segments together for a total of 28 blocks. Trim four blocks to 8½" x 8½". Trim the remaining 24 blocks to 8" x 9".

5. Cut two of the 8½" x 8½" blocks in half diagonally from the lower-right corner to the upper-left corner. Label the four resulting triangles A. Cut the remaining two 8½" blocks in half diagonally from the lower-left corner to the upper-right corner. Label the four resulting triangles B.

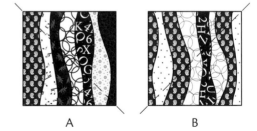

A   B

6. Sew each A triangle to a B triangle along the cut edges to make four border corner blocks. Trim each block to 8" x 8".

Make 4.
Trim to 8" x 8".

ASSEMBLING THE QUILT TOP

1. Arrange the Heart blocks into seven horizontal rows of six blocks each. Alternate the blocks with a red background and the blocks with a white-with-black background in each row and from row to row. Rearrange the blocks until you're satisfied with the layout.

2. Pin and sew the blocks in each row together. Press the seam allowances in alternating directions from row to row. Sew the rows together. Press the seam allowances in one direction.

3. Referring to "Adding Borders" on page 8 and the quilt assembly diagram at right, sew the black 1½"-wide inner-border strips together end to end to make one long strip. Press the seam allowances open. Measure the length of the quilt top through the center and cut two inner-border strips to this measurement. Pin and sew the borders to the sides of the quilt. Press the seam allowances toward the border strips. Measure the width of the quilt top through the center, including the borders just added, and cut two inner-border strips to this measurement. Pin and sew the borders to the top and bottom of the quilt; press the seam allowances toward the border strips.

4. Sew the 8" x 9" Border blocks into two rows of five blocks each for the top and bottom outer-border strips, and two rows of seven blocks each for the side outer-border strips. Press the seam allowances in one direction.

Top/bottom border.
Make 2.

Side border.
Make 2.

5. Refer to "Adding Borders" to trim the top and bottom outer-border strips to the width of the quilt top. Trim the side outer-border strips to the length of the quilt top. Sew the side borders to the sides of the quilt top. Press the seam allowances

toward the inner border. Add a corner border block to the ends of the top and bottom borders, making sure the diagonal seams are directed toward the quilt center. Press the seam allowances toward the border strips. Sew these strips to the top and bottom of the quilt top. Press the seam allowances toward the inner border.

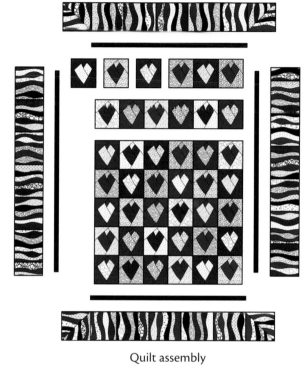

Quilt assembly

FINISHING YOUR QUILT

Refer to "Finishing the Quilt" on page 13 as needed.

1. Divide the backing fabric crosswise into two equal panels, each approximately 63" long. Remove the selvages and sew the pieces together along a long edge to make a backing piece approximately 63" x 80"; press the seam allowance to one side.

2. Layer the quilt top with the batting and backing, keeping the backing seam parallel to the short edges of the quilt top. Baste the layers together using your favorite method.

3. Hand or machine quilt as desired.

4. Trim the backing and batting even with the edges of the quilt top and use the 2½"-wide strips to bind the quilt.

black of diamonds

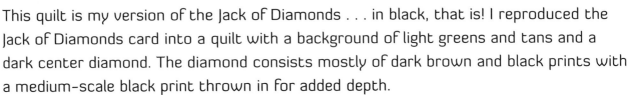

This quilt is my version of the Jack of Diamonds . . . in black, that is! I reproduced the Jack of Diamonds card into a quilt with a background of light greens and tans and a dark center diamond. The diamond consists mostly of dark brown and black prints with a medium-scale black print thrown in for added depth.

Finished Quilt: 60" x 80"

Finished Block: 5¾" x 7¾"

Blocks Needed: 32 pieced and 68 solid

fabric tips

Choose a variety of tan and muted green prints for the background. Make sure each of your choices has a pattern in the print, rather than just appearing as one solid color, so that there's some movement in the prints and they look good together when viewed from a distance. For the large diamond, look for mostly dense, dark prints in black and dark brown.

MATERIALS

⅝ yard *each* of 4 assorted light- to medium-value prints for blocks and outer border

⅓ yard *each* of 3 assorted light- to medium-value prints for blocks and outer border

⅝ yard *each* of 4 assorted dark-brown and/or black prints for blocks

½ yard of dark-red print for inner and outer borders

⅝ yard of fabric for binding

5¼ yards of fabric for backing

68" x 88" piece of batting

CUTTING

From *each* of the 7 assorted light- to medium-value prints, cut:
1 strip, 8¼" x 42"; crosscut into 6 rectangles, 6¼" x 8¼" (42 total)

From the remainder of the assorted light- to medium-value prints, cut a *total* of:
16 rectangles, 7" x 9"

2 rectangles, 6¼" x 8¼"

From *each* of the 4 assorted dark-brown and/or black prints, cut:
1 strip, 9" x 42"; crosscut into 4 rectangles, 7" x 9" (16 total)

1 strip, 8¼" x 42"; crosscut into 6 rectangles, 6¼" x 8¼" (24 total)

From the dark-red print, cut:
8 strips, 1½" x 42"

From the fabric for binding, cut:
7 strips, 2½" x 42"

MAKING THE BLOCKS

Refer to "Stacking the Deck" on pages 9–12 for details as needed.

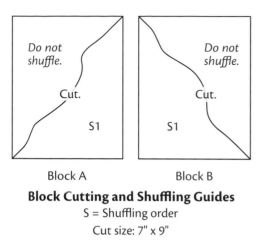

Block A   Block B

Block Cutting and Shuffling Guides
S = Shuffling order
Cut size: 7" x 9"

1. Arrange the 7" x 9" rectangles into 16 decks with one dark-brown or black rectangle and one light-to medium-value rectangle in each deck. Separate the decks into two sets of eight decks each. Label one set of decks A and the other set of decks B.

2. Referring to the block cutting and shuffling guide above, cut the individual decks from set A in half diagonally from the lower-left corner to the upper-right corner using the Creative Grids Curves for Rectangles ruler, or cut the curves free-form by following the instructions in "Cutting Curves" on page 9. Be sure that the first and last 1" of the cutting line are both at a 45° angle to the rectangle edges.

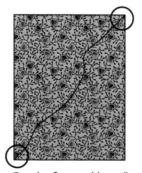

Cut the first and last 1"
of the diagonal line at a 45° angle.

3. Shuffle each deck as indicated on the block cutting and shuffling guide. Secure each shuffled deck to a piece of paper with a pin through all layers until you're ready to sew.

4. Referring to "Sewing Curves" on page 11, sew the shuffled segments together to make two blocks from each deck for a total of 16 A blocks. Press the seam allowances toward the dark-brown or black fabric. Trim each block to 6¼" x 8¼".

Block A

5. Referring to the block cutting and shuffling guide cut the individual decks from set B in half diagonally from the lower-right corner to the upper-left corner using the Creative Grids Curves for Rectangles ruler, or cut the curves free-form by following the instructions in "Cutting Curves" on page 9. Be sure that the first and last 1" of the cutting line are both at a 45° angle to the rectangle edges. If you're using the Curves for Rectangles ruler, simply flip each deck upside down to cut it, and then flip it right side up to sew the blocks. Refer to step 4 to sew the shuffled segments together to make 16 B blocks. Press and trim as for the A blocks.

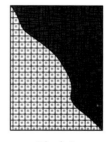

Block B

ASSEMBLING THE QUILT TOP

1. Refer to the quilt assembly diagram at right to arrange the blocks and the light- to medium-value 6¼" x 8¼" rectangles for the quilt center into eight horizontal rows of eight blocks each. Arrange the blocks and rectangles for the border around the center, leaving room for the dark-red strips. Temporarily lay the dark-red strips in place. Rearrange the blocks until you're satisfied with the layout.

2. Pin and sew the blocks in each row of the quilt center together. Press the seam allowance in alternating directions from row to row. Sew the rows together. Press the seam allowances in one direction.

3. Referring to "Adding Borders" on page 8 and the quilt assembly diagram, sew the dark-red 1½"-wide strips together end to end to make one long strip. Press the seam allowances open. Measure the length of the quilt top through the center and cut two inner-border strips to this measurement. Pin and sew the borders to the sides of the quilt. Press the seam allowances toward the border strips.

4. Sew the blocks for each outer side border together. Sew the pieced borders to the sides of the quilt top. Press the seam allowances toward the inner border.

5. Measure the width of the quilt top through the center, including the borders just added. From the remainder of the pieced dark red strip, cut two strips to this measurement. Pin and sew the borders to the top and bottom of the quilt. Press the seam allowances toward the dark-red strips.

6. From the remainder of the pieced dark-red strip, cut four 1½" x 8¼" strips. Sew these strips together with the blocks for the top and bottom outer borders, referring to the quilt assembly diagram as necessary. Press the seam allowances toward

the red strips. Sew these borders to the top and bottom of the quilt top. Press the seam allowances toward the inner-border strips.

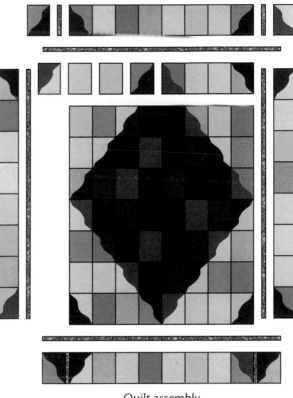

Quilt assembly

FINISHING YOUR QUILT

Refer to "Finishing the Quilt" on page 13 as needed.

1. Divide the backing fabric crosswise into two equal panels, each approximately 88" long. Remove the selvages and sew the pieces together along a long edge to make a backing piece approximately 80" x 88"; press the seam allowance to one side.

2. Layer the quilt top with the batting and backing, keeping the backing seam parallel to the long edges of the quilt top. Baste the layers together using your favorite method.

3. Hand or machine quilt as desired.

4. Trim the backing and batting even with the edges of the quilt top and use the 2½"-wide strips to bind the quilt.

cartwheels

A celebration of earth tones, set in a wavy dance of pinwheels, creates an organic energy with this quilt.

Finished Quilt: 68⅜" x 85⅛"

Finished Block: 7¾" x 7¾"

Blocks Needed: 48

fabric tips

This quilt can be made in any combination of your favorite colors—I chose four lights and four darks that I felt looked good together. Go out on a limb a bit when you choose your colors, and choose prints that have small-scale designs rather than a solid color and still read either light or dark. For the sashing, I chose a deep red that contrasted well with the block colors. The large print in the outer border pulls it all together by using several colors from the blocks.

MATERIALS

⅝ yard *each* of 4 assorted light-tan and light-green prints for blocks

⅝ yard *each* of 4 assorted dark-brown and dark-green prints for blocks

1¾ yards of green print for outer border

1 yard of dark-red print for sashing and inner border

⅝ yard of dark-brown print for middle border

¾ yard of fabric for binding

5½ yards of fabric for backing

77" x 93" piece of batting

CUTTING

From *each* of the 4 assorted light prints, cut:
2 strips, 9" x 42"; crosscut into 6 squares, 9" x 9" (24 total)

From *each* of the 4 assorted dark prints, cut:
2 strips, 9" x 42"; crosscut into 6 squares, 9" x 9" (24 total)

From the dark-red print, cut:
26 strips, 1⅛" x 42"; crosscut *10 of the strips* into 40 strips, 1⅛" x 8¼"

From the dark-brown print, cut:
7 strips, 2½" x 42"

From the green print, cut:
8 strips, 7" x 42"

From the fabric for binding, cut:
9 strips, 2½" x 42"

MAKING THE BLOCKS

Refer to "Stacking the Deck" on pages 9–12 for details as needed.

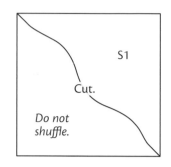

Block Cutting and Shuffling Guide
S = Shuffling order
Cut size: 9" x 9"

1. Arrange the 9" x 9" squares into 12 decks with two light squares and two dark squares in each deck. Alternate the light and dark squares in each deck.

2. Refer to the block cutting and shuffling guide above to cut each deck in half diagonally using the Creative Grids Curves for Squares ruler, or cut the curves free-form by following the instructions in "Cutting Curves" on page 9. Be sure that the first and last 1" of the cutting line are both at a 45° angle to the square edges.

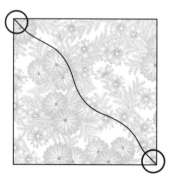

Cut the first and last 1"
of the diagonal line at a 45° angle.

3. Shuffle each deck as indicated on the block cutting and shuffling guide. Secure each shuffled deck to a piece of paper with a pin through all layers until you're ready to sew.

4. Referring to "Sewing Curves" on page 11, sew the shuffled segments together to make four blocks from each deck for a total of 48 blocks. Press the seam allowances toward the dark fabric. Trim the blocks to 8¼" x 8¼".

ASSEMBLING THE QUILT TOP

1. Refer to the assembly diagram on page 27 to arrange the blocks into eight horizontal rows of six blocks each, rotating the blocks to create the design. Rearrange the blocks until you're satisfied with the layout.

2. Place a dark-red 1⅛" x 8¼" vertical sashing strip between the blocks in each row. Sew the blocks and sashing strips in each row together. Press the seam allowances toward the sashing.

3. Refer to "Adding Borders" on page 8 to sew the remaining dark-red strips together end to end to make one long strip. Press the seam allowances open. Measure the block rows through the center. From the pieced strip, cut nine horizontal sashing strips to this measurement. Refer to the assembly diagram to alternately sew the sashing strips and block rows together. Press the seam allowances toward the horizontal sashing.

4. Measure the length of the quilt top through the center. From the remainder of the pieced dark-red strip, cut two inner-border strips to this

measurement. Pin and sew the borders to the sides of the quilt. Press the seam allowances toward the border strips.

5. Sew the dark brown 2½"-wide middle-border strips together end to end to make one long strip. Press the seam allowances open. Measure the length of the quilt top through the center and cut two middle-border strips to this measurement. Pin and sew the borders to the sides of the quilt. Press the seam allowances toward the middle border. Measure the width of the quilt top through the center, including the borders just added, and cut two middle-border strips to this measurement. Pin and sew the borders to the top and bottom of the quilt. Press the seam allowances toward the middle border.

6. Repeat step 5 with the 7"-wide green print strips to add the outer border to the quilt top. Press the seam allowances toward the outer border.

FINISHING YOUR QUILT

Refer to "Finishing the Quilt" on page 13 as needed.

1. Divide the backing crosswise into two equal panels, each approximately 93" long. Remove the selvages and sew the pieces together along a long edge to make a backing piece approximately 80" x 93"; press the seam allowance to one side.

2. Layer the quilt top with the batting and backing, keeping the backing seam parallel to the long edges of the quilt top. Baste the layers together using your favorite method.

3. Hand or machine quilt as desired. My quilt was long-arm quilted.

4. Trim the backing and batting even with the edges of the quilt top and use the 2½"-wide strips to bind the quilt.

Quilt assembly

first dawn

The simple arrangement of wavy pinwheels and solid squares creates a link from the dark center of this quilt to the lighter outer edges, reminding me of morning's first light.

Finished Quilt: 66" x 90"
Finished Block: 12" x 12"
Blocks Needed: 18 Pinwheel and 17 Four Patch

fabric tips

When choosing fabric for this quilt, think simply in terms of light, medium, and dark prints. You'll be choosing four of each value, so you might find it helpful to use my 10-foot rule on page 7. Preview all the fabrics of one value together. Each set of prints should look fairly blended (but not identical) from a distance, but up close each individual fabric will have a different scale or style of print. If you choose prints that appear solid from a distance, be consistent throughout your selection.

MATERIALS

⅞ yard *each* of 4 assorted medium green and turquoise prints for blocks and pieced border

½ yard *each* of 4 assorted light blue, purple, and green prints for blocks

½ yard *each* of 4 assorted dark blue and purple prints for blocks

⅔ yard of fabric for binding

5½ yards of fabric for backing

74" x 98" piece of batting

CUTTING

From *each* of the 4 assorted light prints, cut:
2 strips, 7" x 42"; crosscut into 9 squares, 7" x 7" (36 total)

From *each* of the 4 assorted medium prints, cut:
1 strip, 7" x 42"; crosscut into 5 squares, 7" x 7" (20 total)

3 strips, 6½" x 42"; crosscut into:

> 10 squares, 6½" x 6½" (40 total)
>
> 12 rectangles, 3¼" x 6½" (48 total)
>
> 1 square, 3¼" x 3¼" (4 total)

From *each* of the 4 assorted dark prints, cut:
1 strip, 7" x 42"; crosscut into 4 squares, 7" x 7" (16 total)

1 strip, 6½" x 42"; crosscut into 6 squares, 6½" x 6½" (24 total)

From the remainder of the dark prints, cut a *total* of:
4 squares, 6½" x 6½"

From the fabric for binding, cut:
8 strips, 2½" x 42"

MAKING THE PINWHEEL BLOCKS

Refer to "Stacking the Deck" on pages 9–12 for details as needed.

Block Cutting and Shuffling Guide
S = Shuffling order
Cut size: 7" x 7"

1. Arrange the light and medium 7" x 7" squares into 10 decks with two different light squares and two different dark squares in each deck. Alternate the light and dark squares in each deck. Repeat with the light and dark 7" x 7" squares to make eight decks.

2. Refer to the block cutting and shuffling guide above to cut each deck in half diagonally using the Creative Grids Curves for Squares ruler, or cut the curves free-form by following the instructions in "Cutting Curves" on page 9. Be sure the first and last 1" of the cutting line is at a 45° angle to the square edges.

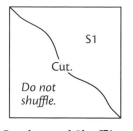

Cut the first and last 1"
of the diagonal line at a 45° angle.

3. Shuffle each deck as indicated on the block cutting and shuffling guide. Secure each deck to a piece of paper with a pin through all layers until ready to sew.

4. Referring to "Sewing Curves" on page 11, sew the shuffled segments together to make four blocks from each deck for a total of 40 light/medium half-square-triangle units and 32 light/dark half-square-triangle units. Press the seam allowances toward the darker fabric. Trim the blocks to 6½" x 6½".

5. Arrange four light/medium half-square-triangle units into two rows of two units each as shown. Sew the units in each row together. Press the seam allowances in alternate directions. Sew the rows together. Press the seam allowances toward the top of the block. Repeat to make a total of 10 light/medium Pinwheel blocks. Repeat with the light/dark half-square-triangle units to make a total of eight Pinwheel blocks.

Make 10.

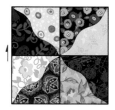

Make 8.

MAKING THE
FOUR PATCH BLOCKS

Arrange the dark 6½" x 6½" squares into two rows of two squares each. Sew the squares in each row together. Press the seam allowances in alternate directions from row to row. Sew the rows together. Press the seam allowance toward the bottom of the block. Repeat to make a total of seven dark blocks. Repeat with the medium 6½" x 6½" squares to make a total of 10 medium blocks.

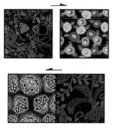 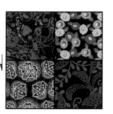

Make 7.

Make 10.

ASSEMBLING THE QUILT TOP

1. Refer to the quilt assembly diagram at right to arrange the Pinwheel and Four Patch blocks into seven horizontal rows of five blocks each as shown. Rearrange the blocks until you're satisfied with the layout, keeping the dark blocks in the center.

2. Arrange 14 medium 3¼" x 6½" rectangles along each side of the quilt top and 10 rectangles along the top and bottom of the quilt top. Add a medium 3¼" square at each corner. When you're satisfied with the arrangement, sew the rectangles together in sets of two each. Press the seam allowance of each set in the opposite direction of the block it's next to. Replace each set in the layout.

3. Pin and sew the pieces in each horizontal row together, including the top and bottom pieced borders. Press the seam allowances in alternating directions from row to row. Pin and sew the rows together. Press the seam allowances in one direction.

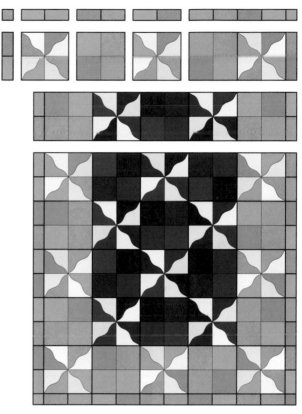

Quilt assembly

FINISHING YOUR QUILT

Refer to "Finishing the Quilt" on page 13 as needed.

1. Divide the backing crosswise into two equal panels, each approximately 98" long. Remove the selvages and sew the pieces together along a long edge to make a backing piece approximately 80" x 98"; press the seam allowance to one side.

2. Layer the quilt top with the batting and backing, keeping the backing seam parallel to the long edges of the quilt top. Baste the layers together using your favorite method.

3. Hand or machine quilt as desired.

4. Trim the backing and batting even with the edges of the quilt top and use the 2½"-wide strips to bind the quilt.

penny lane

Sweet, light small-scale prints mixed with almost-solid turquoise prints make the Half-Square-Triangle blocks that are arranged in a charming layout.

Finished Quilt: 61½" x 77½"

Finished Block: 8" x 8"

Blocks Needed: 48

fabric tips

Choose a mix of three different light-value prints with stripes if available; otherwise, opt for any small-scale prints in a light value. For the turquoise, I chose prints that look almost solid from a distance. Use my 10-foot rule (page 7) to preview your choices. Both the light set and dark set of prints should appear slightly blended when previewed in their own group. But make sure they're different enough from each other to create an interesting mix when they're used in the quilt.

MATERIALS

⅝ yard *each* of 3 assorted turquoise prints for blocks

⅝ yard *each* of 3 assorted light small-scale striped prints for blocks

1½ yards of turquoise print for outer border

⅓ yard of sandy-brown print for inner border

⅔ yard of fabric for binding

4⅞ yards of fabric for backing

70" x 86" piece of batting

CUTTING

From *each* of the 3 assorted turquoise prints, cut:
2 strips, 9" x 42"; crosscut into 8 squares, 9" x 9" (24 total)

From *each* of the 3 assorted light prints, cut:
2 strips, 9" x 42"; crosscut into 8 squares, 9" x 9" (24 total)

From the sandy-brown print, cut:
6 strips, 1½" x 42"

From the turquoise print for outer border, cut:
8 strips, 6" x 42"

From the fabric for binding, cut:
8 strips, 2½" x 42"

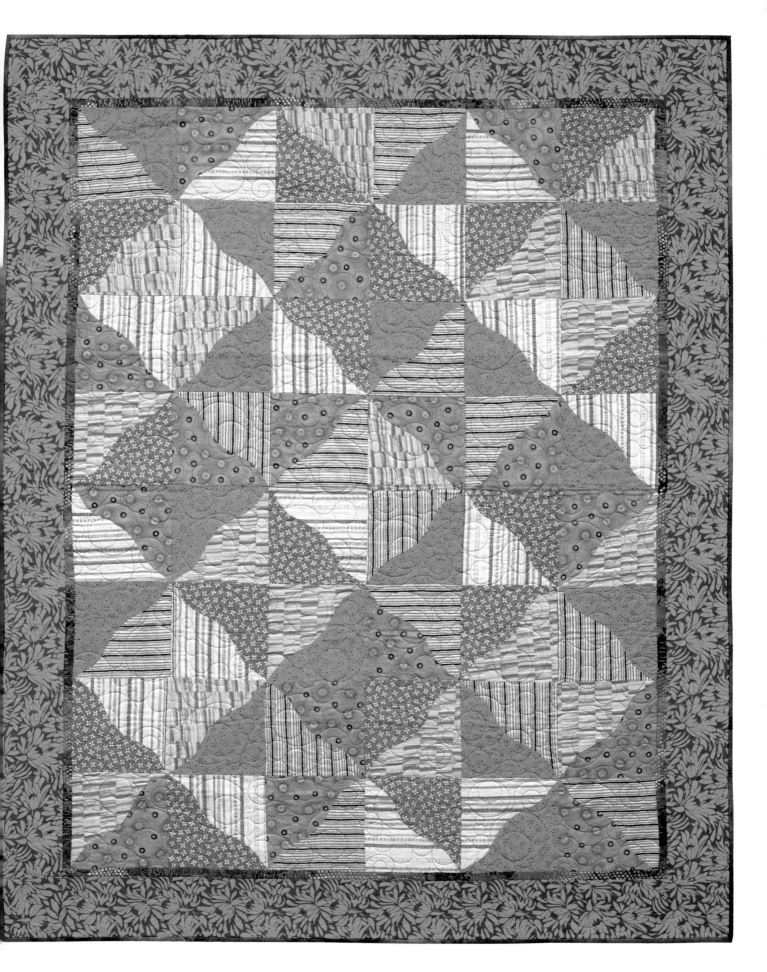

MAKING THE BLOCKS

Refer to "Stacking the Deck" on pages 9–12 for details as needed.

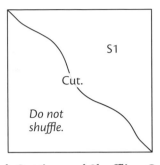

Block Cutting and Shuffling Guide
S = Shuffling order
Cut size: 9" x 9"

1. Arrange the 9" x 9" squares into 12 decks with two different light squares and two different turquoise squares in each deck. Alternate the light and turquoise squares in each deck.

2. Refer to the block cutting and shuffling guide above to cut each deck in half diagonally using the Creative Grids Curves for Squares ruler, or cut the curves free-form by following the instructions in "Cutting Curves" on page 9. Be sure that the first and last 1" of the cutting line are both at a 45° angle to the square edges.

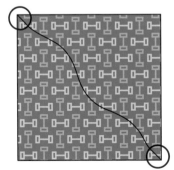

Cut the first and last 1"
of the diagonal line at a 45° angle.

3. Shuffle each deck as indicated on the block cutting and shuffling guide. Secure each shuffled deck to a piece of paper with a pin through all layers until you're ready to sew.

4. Referring to "Sewing Curves" on page 11, sew the shuffled segments together to make four blocks from each deck for a total of 48 blocks. Press the seam allowances toward the turquoise fabric. Trim each block to 8½" x 8½".

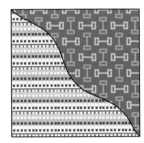

ASSEMBLING THE QUILT TOP

1. Refer to the quilt assembly diagram on page 35 to arrange the blocks into eight horizontal rows of six blocks each. Pay careful attention to how each block is rotated. Rearrange the blocks until you're satisfied with the layout.

2. Pin and sew the blocks in each row together. Press the seam allowances in alternating directions from row to row. Sew the rows together. Press the seam allowances in one direction.

jumbo blocks

Sometimes it's easier to combine the blocks into jumbo blocks first, and then assemble your quilt top. For this quilt, you would make four horizontal rows of three jumbo blocks each.

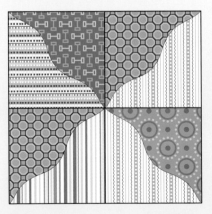

3. Refer to "Adding Borders" on page 8 and the quilt assembly diagram to sew the sandy-brown 1½"-wide inner-border strips together end to end to make one long strip. Measure the length of the quilt top through the center and cut two inner-border strips to this measurement. Pin and sew the borders to the sides of the quilt. Press the seam allowances toward the border strips. Measure the width of the quilt top through the center, including the borders just added, and cut two inner-border strips to this measurement. Pin and sew the borders to the top and bottom of the quilt. Press the seam allowances toward the border strips.

4. Repeat step 3 with the turquoise 6"-wide strips to add the outer border to the quilt top. Press the seam allowances toward the outer border.

FINISHING YOUR QUILT

Refer to "Finishing the Quilt" on page 13 as needed.

1. Divide the backing crosswise into two equal panels, each approximately 86" long. Remove the selvages and sew the pieces together along a long edge to make a backing piece approximately 80" x 86"; press the seam allowance to one side.

2. Layer the quilt top with the batting and backing, keeping the backing seam parallel to the long edges of the quilt top. Baste the layers together using your favorite method.

3. Hand or machine quilt as desired.

4. Trim the backing and batting even with the edges of the quilt top and use the 2½"-wide strips to bind the quilt.

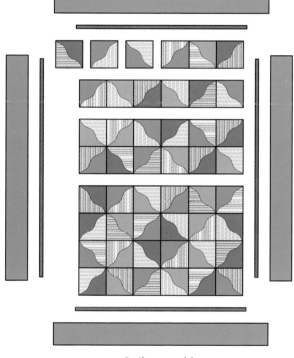

Quilt assembly

BIV

This little quilt contains a lot of my favorite colors—so many, in fact, that I named it "BIV," which stands for blue, indigo, and violet.

Finished Quilt: 49½" x 61½"

Finished Block: 12" x 12"

Blocks Needed: 12

fabric tips

I went through my stash of blues, indigos, and violets in order to make a no-holds-barred blue quilt. I encourage you to do the same using one of your favorite colors.

MATERIALS

¼ yard *each* of 6 assorted dark prints ranging from purple to dark blue

¼ yard *each* of 6 assorted medium prints ranging from turquoise to blue

1⅛ yards of medium-blue print for border

½ yard of fabric for binding

3⅓ yards of fabric for backing

58" x 70" piece of batting

CUTTING

From *each* of the 6 assorted medium prints, cut:
1 strip, 7" x 42"; crosscut into 4 rectangles, 7" x 9" (24 total)

From *each* of the 6 assorted dark prints, cut:
1 strip, 7" x 42"; crosscut into 4 rectangles, 7" x 9" (24 total)

From the medium-blue print for border, cut:
5 strips, 7" x 42"

From the fabric for binding, cut:
6 strips, 2½" x 42"

MAKING THE BLOCKS

Refer to "Stacking the Deck" on pages 9–12 for details as needed.

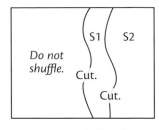

Block Cutting and Shuffling Guide
S = Shuffling order
Cut size: 7" x 9"

1. Arrange the medium and dark 7" x 9" rectangles into 12 decks with two different medium prints and two different dark prints in each deck. Alternate the medium and dark prints in each deck.

2. Refer to the block cutting and shuffling guide above to cut each deck using the Creative Grids Curved Slotted ruler, or cut the curves free-form by following the instructions in "Cutting Curves" on page 9. If you are using the ruler, choose different slots for each cut.

3. Shuffle each deck as indicated on the block cutting and shuffling guide. Secure each shuffled deck to a piece of paper with a pin through all layers until you're ready to sew.

4. Referring to "Sewing Curves" on page 11, sew the shuffled segments together to make two light and two dark pieced rectangles from each deck for a total of 48. Press the seam allowances in one direction. Trim the rectangles to 6½" x 6½".

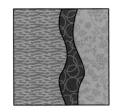

5. Group the pieced squares into six sets of four light squares and six sets of four dark squares. Arrange the squares in each set into two horizontal rows of two squares each, rotating the curved stripe as shown. Sew the squares in each row together. Press the seam allowances as indicated for each set. Sew the rows together. Press the seam allowances as indicated for each set.

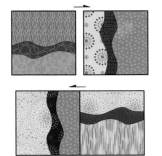
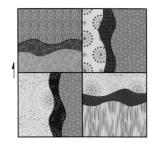

Make 6.

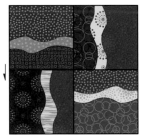

Make 6.

ASSEMBLING THE QUILT TOP

1. Refer to the quilt assembly diagram on page 39 to arrange the blocks into four horizontal rows of three blocks each, alternating the light and dark blocks in each row and from row to row. Rearrange the blocks until you're satisfied with the layout.

2. Pin and sew the blocks in each row together. Press the seam allowances in alternating directions from row to row. Sew the rows together. Press the seam allowances in one direction.

3. Referring to "Adding Borders" on page 8, sew the 7"-wide medium-blue border strips together end to end to make one long strip. Press the seam allowances open. Measure the length of the quilt top through the center and cut two border strips to this measurement. Pin and sew the borders to the sides of the quilt. Press the seam allowances toward the border strips. Measure the width of the quilt top through the center, including the borders just added, and cut two border strips to this measurement. Pin and sew the borders to the top and bottom of the quilt. Press the seam allowances toward the border strips.

FINISHING YOUR QUILT

Refer to "Finishing the Quilt" on page 13 as needed.

1. Divide the backing crosswise into two equal panels, each approximately 58" long. Remove the selvages and sew the pieces together along a long edge to make a backing piece approximately 58" x 80"; press the seam allowance to one side.

2. Layer the quilt top with the batting and backing, keeping the backing seam parallel to the short edges of the quilt top. Baste the layers together using your favorite method.

3. Hand or machine quilt as desired.

4. Trim the backing and batting even with the edges of the quilt top and use the 2½"-wide strips to bind the quilt.

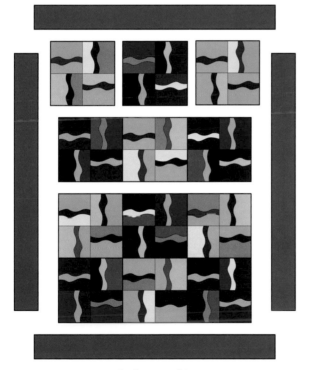

Quilt assembly

diamondback

The blocks in this quilt are a lot of fun to make and create very interesting diamond patterns when arranged together. The design lends itself well to the intense colors found in most batiks.

Finished Quilt: 59½" x 75½"

Finished Block: 6" x 8"

Blocks Needed: 64

fabric tips

Batiks seemed like the perfect choice for this quilt. Their deep colors seem to really accentuate the diamonds, and the mottled variation of colors found in batiks keeps the eye moving. Preview your fabric choices, making sure you like the transition from one color group to the next. You'll have extra fabric from the dark brown prints. If you don't mind the repeat of prints you could use fewer fabrics. I like mixing more prints, so I chose five different batiks.

MATERIALS

⅓ yard *each* of 5 assorted dark-brown batiks for blocks

⅓ yard *each* of 5 assorted medium-brown batiks for blocks

⅓ yard *each* of 4 assorted lime and yellowish-green batiks for blocks

1⅓ yards of dark-brown batik for border

½ yard of a different medium-brown batik for blocks

⅝ yard of fabric for binding

4¾ yards of fabric for backing

68" x 84" piece of batting

CUTTING

From *each* of the 4 assorted lime and yellowish-green batiks, cut:
1 strip, 9" x 42"; crosscut into 5 rectangles, 7" x 9" (20 total; you'll have 2 left over)

From *each* of the 5 assorted medium-brown batiks (⅓-yard cuts), cut:
1 strip, 9" x 42"; crosscut into 5 rectangles, 7" x 9" (25 total)

From the ½-yard cut of medium-brown batik, cut:
2 strips, 9" x 42"; crosscut into 7 rectangles, 7" x 9"

From *each* of the 5 assorted dark-brown batiks, cut:
1 strip, 9" x 42"; crosscut into 3 rectangles, 7" x 9" (15 total; you'll have 1 left over)

From the dark-brown batik for border, cut:
7 strips, 6" x 42"

From the fabric for binding, cut:
7 strips, 2½" x 42"

MAKING THE BLOCKS

Refer to "Stacking the Deck" on pages 9–12 as needed.

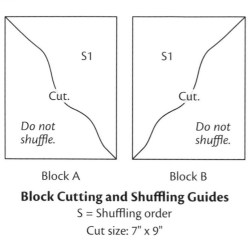

Block Cutting and Shuffling Guides
S = Shuffling order
Cut size: 7" x 9"

1. Arrange the 7" x 9" rectangles into the following decks: eight decks, alternating two green and two medium-brown rectangles in each; two decks with one green and one medium-brown rectangle in each; six decks, alternating two medium-brown and two dark-brown rectangles in each; two decks with one medium-brown and one dark-brown rectangle in each.

2. Referring to the block cutting and shuffling guides above, cut half of the decks of each color combination in half diagonally from the lower-right corner to the upper-left corner using the Creative Grids Curves for Rectangles ruler, or cut the curves free-form by following the instructions in "Cutting Curves" on page 9. Be sure that the first and last 1" of the cutting line are both at a 45° angle to the rectangle edges. Label these decks A. Cut the remaining decks in half diagonally from the lower-left corner to the upper-right corner as described

for the A decks. If you are using the ruler, simply flip each deck upside down to cut it, and then flip it right side up before sewing. Label these decks B.

Cut the first and last 1"
of the diagonal line at a 45° angle.

3. Shuffle each deck as indicated on the block cutting and shuffling guide. Secure each shuffled deck to a piece of paper with a pin through all layers until you're ready to sew.

4. Referring to "Sewing Curves" on page 11, sew the shuffled segments together to make 18 each of the green-and-medium-brown A and B blocks and 14 each of the medium-brown and dark-brown A and B blocks. Press the seam allowances toward the darker fabric. Trim each block to 6½" x 8½".

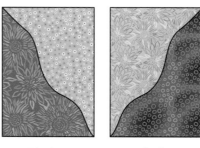

Block A   Block B
Make 18 of each.

Block A   Block B
Make 14 of each.

ASSEMBLING THE QUILT TOP

1. Refer to the quilt assembly diagram below to arrange the blocks into eight horizontal rows of eight blocks each. Rearrange the blocks until you're satisfied with the layout, making sure to maintain the design if you switch blocks.

2. Pin and sew the blocks in each row together. Press the seam allowances in alternating directions from row to row. Sew the rows together. Press the seam allowances in one direction.

3. Refer to "Adding Borders" on page 8 to sew the border strips together end to end to make one long strip. Press the seam allowances open. Measure the length of the quilt top through the center and cut two border strips to this measurement. Pin and sew the borders to the sides of the quilt. Press the seam allowances toward the border strips. Measure the width of the quilt top through the center, including the borders just added, and cut two border strips to this measurement. Pin and sew the borders to the top and bottom of the quilt. Press the seam allowances toward the border strips.

FINISHING YOUR QUILT

Refer to "Finishing the Quilt" on page 13 as needed.

1. Divide the backing crosswise into two equal panels, each approximately 84" long. Remove the selvages and sew the pieces together along a long edge to make a backing piece approximately 80" x 84"; press the seam allowance to one side.

2. Layer the quilt top with the batting and backing, keeping the backing seam parallel to the long edges of the quilt top. Baste the layers together using your favorite method.

3. Hand or machine quilt as desired.

4. Trim the backing and batting even with the edges of the quilt top and use the 2½"-wide strips to bind the quilt.

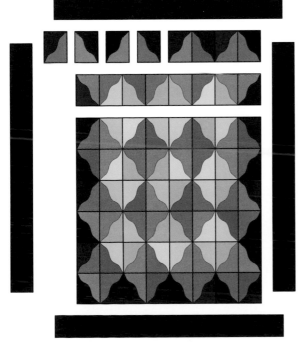

Quilt assembly

wavelength

This bright quilt begins with a warm palette set in a mix of soft background colors. Little Square-in-a-Square blocks spring through the large zigzags that wander horizontally across the quilt top, reminding me of wavelengths.

Finished Quilt: 63½" x 86"

Finished Blocks: 9" x 9" and 4½" x 4½"

Blocks Needed: 36 Half-Square-Triangle and 72 Square-in-a-Square

fabric tips

While I chose a warm color theme for this quilt, you could just as easily use a cool palette to simulate ocean waves if you'd like. Choose five dark fabrics with three or more colors in each. My rule was to avoid using any white in the prints in this group. For the lights, I chose mainly airy prints filled with many colors on a white background, and then I tossed in a couple of colorful prints on a turquoise background.

MATERIALS

1 yard *each* of 5 assorted light prints for blocks and border

¾ yard *each* of 5 assorted dark red and orange prints for blocks

⅔ yard of fabric for binding

5¼ yards of fabric for backing

70" x 92" piece of batting

CUTTING

From *each* of the 5 assorted dark prints, cut:
1 strip, 10" x 42"; crosscut into 4 squares, 10" x 10" (20 total; you'll have 2 left over)

2 strips, 6" x 42"; crosscut into 8 squares, 6" x 6" (40 total; you'll have 4 left over)

From *each* of the 5 assorted light prints, cut:
1 strip, 10" x 42"; crosscut into 4 squares, 10" x 10" (20 total; you'll have 2 left over)

2 strips, 6" x 42"; crosscut into 8 squares, 6" x 6" (40 total; you'll have 4 left over)

2 strips, 5" x 42"; crosscut into:

4 rectangles, 5" x 9½" (20 total; you'll have 4 left over)

4 squares, 5" x 5" (20 total; you'll have 2 left over)

From the fabric for binding, cut:
8 strips, 2½" x 42"

MAKING THE HALF-SQUARE-TRIANGLE BLOCKS

Refer to "Stacking the Deck" on pages 9–12 as needed.

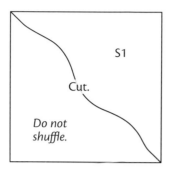

Block Cutting and Shuffling Guide
S = Shuffling order
Cut size: 10" x 10"

1. Arrange the 10" x 10" squares into nine decks with two different light squares and two different dark squares in each deck. Alternate the light and dark squares in each deck.

2. Referring to the block cutting and shuffling guide above, cut each deck in half diagonally using the Creative Grids Curves for Squares ruler, or cut the curves free-form by following the instructions in "Cutting Curves" on page 9. Be sure that the first and last 1" of the cutting line are both at a 45° angle to the square edges.

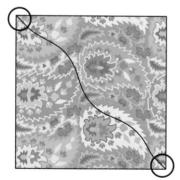

Cut the first and last 1"
of the diagonal line at a 45° angle.

3. Shuffle each deck as indicated on the block cutting and shuffling guide. Secure each shuffled deck to a piece of paper with a pin through all layers until ready to sew.

4. Referring to "Sewing Curves" on page 11, sew the shuffled segments together to make four blocks from each deck for a total of 36 blocks. Press the seam allowances toward the dark fabric. Trim each block to 9½" x 9½".

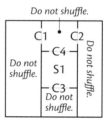

MAKING THE SQUARE-IN-A-SQUARE BLOCKS

Refer to "Stacking the Deck" on pages 9–12 as needed.

Block Cutting and Shuffling Guide
C = Cutting order
S = Shuffling order
Cut size: 6" x 6"

1. Arrange the 6" x 6" squares into 12 decks with three different light squares and three different dark squares in each deck. Alternate the light and dark squares in each deck.

2. Refer to the block cutting and shuffling guide above to cut each deck. Cut each deck slightly different from one to the next. Make sure none of your cuts results in a piece that is less than 1" wide.

3. Shuffle each deck as indicated on the block cutting and shuffling guide. Secure each shuffled deck to a piece of paper with a pin through all layers until you're ready to sew.

4. Chain sew the three center sections for each deck together. Press the seam allowances toward the dark fabric. Add the two outer pieces to each center segment; the outer pieces will be approximately 1" longer than the center. Trim the edges flush with the center section. Trim the blocks to 5" x 5". Make 36 light blocks and 36 dark blocks.

Trim excess.

Make 36.   Make 36.

ASSEMBLING THE QUILT TOP

1. Refer to the quilt assembly diagram at right to arrange 36 of the Half-Square-Triangle blocks, all of the dark Square-in-a-Square blocks, and 24 of the light Square-in-a-Square blocks into horizontal rows as shown. Rearrange the blocks until you're satisfied with the layout. Next, arrange the border pieces around the center, using the remaining light Square-in-a-Square blocks, the light 5" squares, and the light 5" x 9½" rectangles. Again, rearrange the pieces until you're satisfied with the layout.

2. Sew the pieces for the side, top, and bottom borders together. Press the seam allowances in one direction.

3. Pin and then sew the blocks in each row together, carefully matching the points of the Half-Square-Triangle blocks. Press the seam allowances in alternate directions from row to row. Sew the rows together. Press the seam allowances in one direction.

4. Join the side borders to the quilt top. Press the seam allowances toward the border strips. Sew the top and bottom borders to the quilt top. Press the seam allowances toward the border strips.

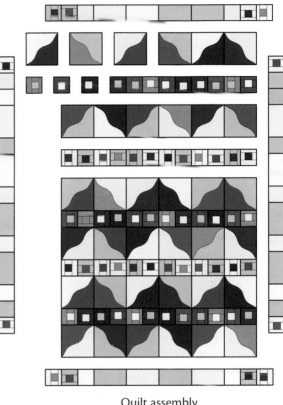

Quilt assembly

FINISHING YOUR QUILT

Refer to "Finishing the Quilt" on page 13 as needed.

1. Divide the backing crosswise into two equal panels, each approximately 92" long. Remove the selvages and sew the pieces together along a long edge to make a backing piece approximately 80" x 92"; press the seam allowance to one side.

2. Layer the quilt top with the batting and backing, keeping the backing seam parallel to the long edges of the quilt top. Baste the layers together using your favorite method.

3. Hand or machine quilt as desired.

4. Trim the backing and batting even with the edges of the quilt top and use the 2½"-wide strips to bind the quilt.

bounce

Playful balls bounce through the wavy blocks, bringing this quilt to life. The placement of the balls is up to you, and you can use as many or as few as you'd like!

Finished Quilt: 51" x 77"

Finished Block: 9" x 9"

Blocks Needed: 24 pieced and 15 solid

---

fabric tips

Choose a variety of lights and darks for the backgrounds of the bouncing balls. I used batiks, but other fabrics would work as well. The unpieced background blocks should appear as solids from a distance so that they don't argue with the fabrics selected for the balls. The balls should be made of bright, contrasting prints and can also duplicate some of the fabrics from the background blocks. Tone-on-tone prints work best. If you have a stash, it's fun to check it out and use a bunch of different prints for the balls. I dove into my stash more than once, so if you see more different fabrics than the materials list calls for, that's why.

MATERIALS

1⅛ yards *each* of 4 assorted light-value tone-on-tone batiks in blues and beiges for blocks

1⅛ yards *each* of 4 assorted dark-value tone-on-tone batiks in purples and blues for blocks

⅓ yard *each* or fat quarters of 4 assorted golden-yellow batiks, 4 assorted red batiks, 4 assorted lime-green batiks, and 4 assorted medium-blue batiks for balls

⅝ yard of fabric for binding

4⅞ yards of fabric for backing

60" x 85" piece of batting

2 yards of lightweight fusible web

CUTTING

From *each* of the 4 assorted dark batiks, cut:
1 strip, 10½" x 42"; crosscut into 3 squares, 10½" x 10½" (12 total)

1 strip, 9½" x 42"; crosscut into 1 square, 9½" x 9½" (4 total)

From the remainder of the assorted dark batiks, cut a *total* of:
3 squares, 14½" x 14½"; cut each square into quarters diagonally to yield 12 side setting triangles (you'll have 2 left over)

3 squares, 9½" x 9½"

From *each* of the 4 assorted light batiks, cut:
1 strip, 10½" x 42"; crosscut into 3 squares, 10½" x 10½" (12 total)

1 strip, 9½" x 42"; crosscut into 2 squares, 9½" x 9½" (8 total)

From the remainder of the assorted light batiks, cut a *total* of:
2 squares, 14½" x 14½"; cut each square into quarters diagonally to yield 8 side setting triangles (you'll have 2 left over)

2 squares, 7½" x 7½"; cut each square in half diagonally to yield 4 corner setting triangles

From the fabric for binding, cut:
7 strips, 2½" x 42"

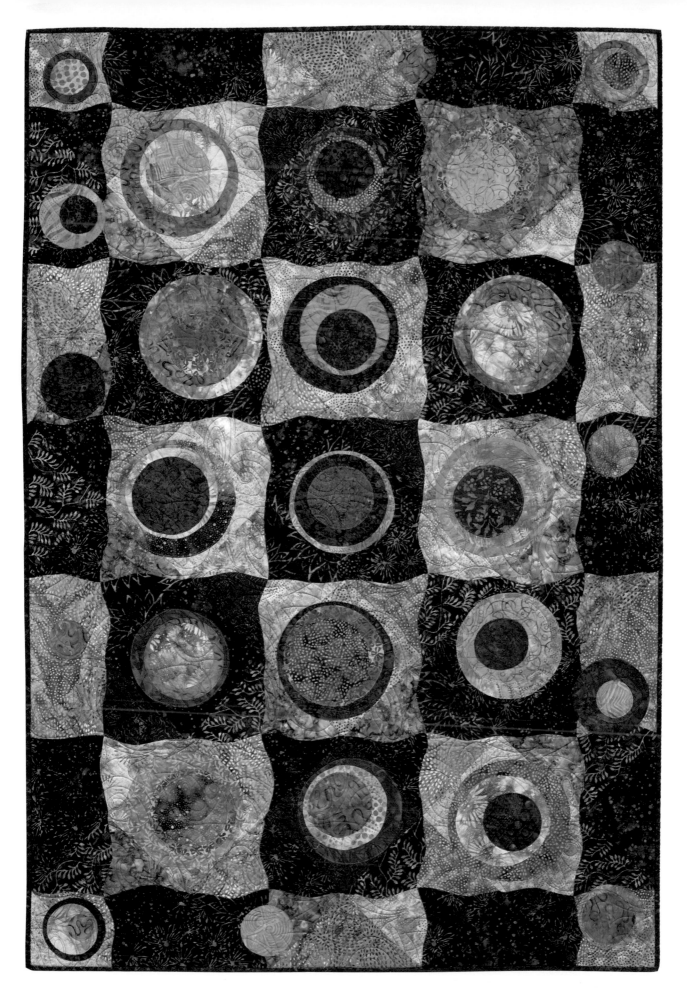

MAKING THE BLOCKS

Refer to "Stacking the Deck" on pages 9–12 as needed.

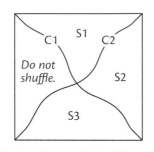

Block Cutting and Shuffling Guide
C = Cutting order
S = Shuffling order
Cut size: 10½" x 10½"

1. Arrange the 10½" x 10½" squares into six decks with two different light squares and two different dark squares in each deck. Alternate the light and dark prints in each deck.

2. Refer to the block cutting and shuffling guide above to cut each deck into quarters using the Creative Grids Curves for Squares ruler, or cut the curves free-form by following the instructions in "Cutting Curves" on page 9. Be sure that the first and last 1" of the cutting line are both at a 45° angle to the square edges and that the center cuts cross at a 90° angle.

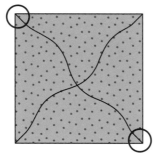

Cut the first and last 1"
of the diagonal line at a 45° angle.

3. Shuffle each deck as indicated on the block cutting and shuffling guide. Secure each shuffled deck to a piece of paper with a pin through all layers until you're ready to sew.

4. Referring to "Sewing Curves" on page 11, sew the shuffled segments together to make four blocks from each deck for a total of 24 blocks as shown, above right. Press the seam allowances in alternate directions. Trim each block to 9½" x 9½".

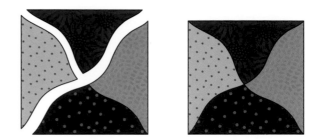

ASSEMBLING THE QUILT TOP

1. Arrange the blocks and the light and dark 9½" squares into diagonal rows as shown. Add the side and corner setting triangles to the ends of the rows. Rearrange like blocks and triangles until you're satisfied with the layout. Do not sew the rows together yet.

2. Make full-size templates of the patterns on page 51. To do this, fold a square of freezer paper that is slightly larger than the finished diameter of the circle into quarters. Align the folds of the paper with the straight lines of the pattern, matching centers. Trace around the curved edge of the pattern. Cut out the freezer-paper pattern along the curved line to create a circle.

3. Working with one solid square at a time, determine which ball sizes you'll use and then select your fabric for each circle. I used circles in three different sizes and three different fabrics, but you can do more or less. Using the full-size circle templates and referring to "Fusible-Web Appliqué"

(page 7) and the photo (page 49) as needed, trace the ball sizes onto fusible web. Cut away the fusible web inside each circle, leaving about 1" inside the marked line for fusing. Fuse the fusible-web circle to the desired fabric and cut it out on the marked line. Remove the paper backing from all but the largest circle.

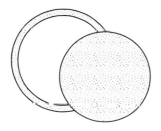

4. Fuse the smaller circles to the largest circle, working from the bottom to the top. After each appliqué is fused in place, cut away the unfused background fabric under the circle before applying the next one. You can use the cut-away fabric to cut more circles. Remove the paper backing from the largest circle and then stitch around the edges of the circles on top of it to secure them. Pin the stacked circle appliqué to the intended square. Repeat for all of the solid squares.

5. Working with one diagonal row at a time, remove the appliqué stacks and make a note of their location in the row. Pin and sew the blocks, squares, and setting triangles in the row together. Press the seam allowances in opposite directions from row to row. Replace the appliqués. Once you get a couple of rows completed, sew the rows together. Remove the paper backing from the large circles and appliqué the circle stacks in place in the general area of the solid squares, overlapping them onto the pieced blocks as desired. Continue sewing the rows together and appliquéing the circle stacks in place until all the rows are joined. Add the corner triangles to the quilt top. Press the seam allowances toward the corners. The setting blocks were cut oversized, so you'll need to trim the quilt-top edges to a

minimum of ¼" from the block points, keeping the distance consistent on each side.

6. Referring to steps 3 and 4 and the photo as needed, create stacks of circle appliqués for the setting triangles; fuse and stitch them in place.

FINISHING YOUR QUILT

Refer to "Finishing the Quilt" on page 13 as needed.

1. Divide the backing crosswise into two equal panels, each approximately 85" long. Remove the selvages and sew the pieces together along a long edge to make a backing piece approximately 80" x 85"; press the seam allowance to one side.

2. Layer the quilt top with the batting and backing, keeping the backing seam parallel to the long edges of the quilt top. Baste the layers together using your favorite method.

3. Hand or machine quilt as desired.

4. Trim the backing and batting even with the edges of the quilt top and use the 2½"-wide strips to bind the quilt.

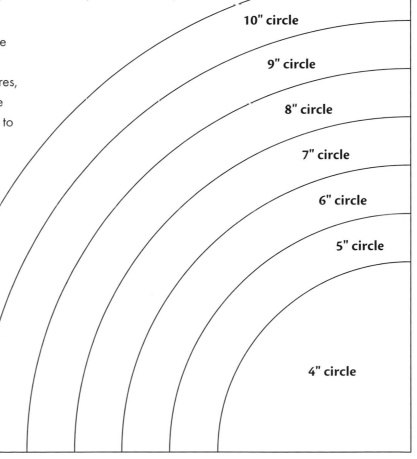

10" circle

9" circle

8" circle

7" circle

6" circle

5" circle

4" circle

pisa

In the fall of 2010, I had the pleasure of climbing the Leaning Tower of Pisa. One thing that really amazed me was the worn marble steps leading to the top of the tower. From repeated journeys to the top and back, the stairs are heavily worn and appear wavy. The higher you climb, the steeper they get. This quilt is my representation of Pisa's famous leaning landmark.

Finished Quilt: 55½" x 75"

Finished Block: 4½" x 5½"

Blocks Needed: 84

fabric tips

Choose mottled prints that appear as solids from a distance. I think batiks work best for this quilt.

MATERIALS

¼ yard *each* of 6 assorted light tone-on-tone batiks in beiges, light greens, and pinks for blocks

¼ yard *each* of 6 assorted medium tone-on-tone batiks in grays for blocks

⅜ yard *each* of 4 assorted dark tone-on-tone batiks in deep turquoises and/or bluish grays for blocks

⅔ yard of medium-brown batik for background

1⅓ yards of dark-brown batik for border

⅝ yard of fabric for binding

4¾ yards of fabric for backing

64" x 83" piece of batting

CUTTING

From the 6 assorted light batiks, cut a *total* of:

18 rectangles, 5½" x 7"

3 rectangles, 3" x 6"

7 rectangles, 4" x 6"

4 rectangles, 5" x 6"

From *each* of the 6 assorted medium batiks, cut:

1 strip, 7" x 42"; crosscut into 6 rectangles, 5½" x 7" (36 total)

From the 4 assorted dark batiks, cut a *total* of:

18 rectangles, 5½" x 7"

3 rectangles, 3" x 6"

7 rectangles, 4" x 6"

4 rectangles, 5" x 6"

From the medium-brown batik, cut:

2 strips, 7" x 42"; crosscut into 12 rectangles, 5½" x 7"

1 strip, 6" x 42"; crosscut into:

    4 rectangles, 5" x 6"

    2 rectangles, 4" x 6"

    2 rectangles, 3" x 6"

From the dark-brown batik, cut:

7 strips, 6" x 42"

From the fabric for binding, cut:

7 strips, 2½" x 42"

MAKING THE BLOCKS

Refer to "Stacking the Deck" on pages 9–12 for details as needed.

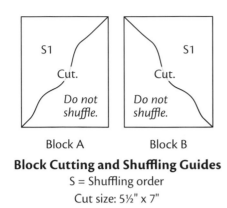

Block A Block B

Block Cutting and Shuffling Guides
S = Shuffling order
Cut size: 5½" x 7"

1. Arrange 15 light and 15 medium 5½" x 7" rectangles into six decks with two different light rectangles and two different medium rectangles in each deck, and one deck with three different light rectangles and three different medium rectangles. Alternate the light and medium rectangles in each deck.

2. Referring to the block A cutting and shuffling guide above, cut each deck in half diagonally from the lower-left corner to the upper-right corner using the Creative Grids Curves for Rectangles ruler, or cut the curves free-form by following the instructions in "Cutting Curves" on page 9. If you are using the ruler, simply flip each deck upside down to cut it, and then flip it right side up before sewing. Be sure that the first and last 1" of the cutting line are both at a 45° angle to the rectangle edges.

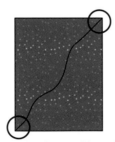

Cut the first and last 1"
of the diagonal line at a 45° angle.

3. Shuffle each deck as indicated on the block cutting and shuffling guide. Secure each shuffled deck to a piece of paper with a pin through all layers until you're ready to sew.

4. Referring to "Sewing Curves" on page 11, sew the shuffled segments together to make a total of 30 light/medium blocks. Press the seam allowances toward the medium fabric.

Block A

5. Arrange 15 medium and 15 dark 5½" x 7" rectangles into six decks with two different medium rectangles and two different dark rectangles in each deck, and one deck with three different medium rectangles and three different dark rectangles. Alternate the medium and dark rectangles in each deck.

6. Referring to the block B cutting and shuffling guide at right, cut each deck in half diagonally from the lower-right corner to the upper-left corner using the Creative Grids Curves for Rectangles ruler, or cut the curves free-form by following the instructions in "Cutting Curves" on page 9. Be sure that the first and last 1" of the cutting line are both at a 45° angle to the rectangle edges.

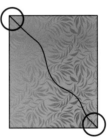

Cut the first and last 1"
of the diagonal line at a 45° angle.

7. Repeat steps 3 and 4 to make a total of 30 medium/dark blocks. Press the seam allowances toward the dark fabric.

Block B

8. Arrange three different light and three different medium-brown 5½" x 7" rectangles into one deck, alternating the light and medium-brown rectangles. Refer to steps 2–4 to cut the deck following the block A diagram, shuffle the segments, and sew the segments together to make six light/medium-brown blocks. Press the seam allowances toward the dark-brown fabric.

9. Arrange six medium rectangles and six medium-brown rectangles into two decks of three different medium rectangles and three brown rectangles. Alternate the medium and brown rectangles in each deck. Cut one deck in half diagonally following the block A diagram and the other block in half diagonally following the block B diagram. Shuffle and sew the blocks together as before to make six medium/brown A blocks and six medium/brown B blocks.

10. Arrange three different dark rectangles and three medium-brown rectangles into one deck, alternating the dark and brown rectangles. Cut the deck in half diagonally following the block B diagram. Shuffle and sew the blocks together as before to make six dark/brown blocks. Press the seam allowances toward the brown fabric.

11. Trim the blocks to 5" x 6".

ASSEMBLING THE QUILT TOP

1. Refer to the quilt assembly diagram to arrange the blocks and the light, dark, and medium-brown rectangles into horizontal rows. Rearrange blocks and rectangles of the same color combination, value, and size until you're satisfied with the layout.

2. Pin and sew the blocks in each row together. Press the seam allowances in alternating directions from row to row. Sew the rows together. Press the seam allowances in one direction.

jumbo blocks

Sometimes it's easier to combine the blocks into jumbo blocks first, and then assemble your quilt top. For this quilt, you would make three horizontal rows of four jumbo blocks each, and two horizontal rows of three jumbo blocks each.

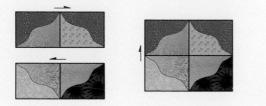

3. Referring to "Adding Borders" on page 8, sew the dark-brown 6"-wide border strips together end to end to make one long strip. Press the seam allowances open. Measure the length of the quilt top through the center and cut two border strips to this measurement. Pin and sew the borders to the sides of the quilt. Press the seam allowances toward the border strips. Measure the width of the quilt top through the center, including the borders just added, and cut two border strips to this measurement. Pin and sew the borders to the top and bottom of the quilt. Press the seam allowances toward the border strips.

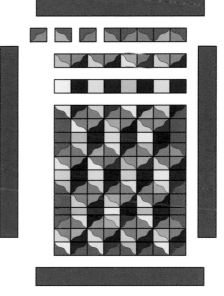

Quilt assembly

FINISHING YOUR QUILT

Refer to "Finishing the Quilt" on page 13 as needed.

1. Divide the backing crosswise into two equal panels, each approximately 83" long. Remove the selvages and sew the pieces together along a long edge to make a backing piece approximately 80" x 83"; press the seam allowance to one side.

2. Layer the quilt top with the batting and backing, keeping the backing seam parallel to the long edges of the quilt top. Baste the layers together using your favorite method.

3. Hand or machine quilt as desired.

4. Trim the backing and batting even with the edges of the quilt top and use the 2½"-wide strips to bind the quilt.

village news

A collection of solid fabrics is perfect for stitching together this modern-looking quilt. The blocks are oversized and a lot of fun to make. This block design can incorporate any group of fabrics, and they always shrink up equally, which is why I call it the No Matter What block—no matter what size square you begin with, you'll always lose an even 2". Once the blocks are pieced, they'll be split into quarters. It might seem a bit daunting at first when you're cutting away, but it will make sense once you get started.

Finished Quilt: 55" x 69½"

Finished Block: 13½" x 13½"

Blocks Needed: 12

---

fabric tips

I picked a mix of solid blues, greens, turquoises, gray, and off-whites for this quilt. If you prefer to use prints, look for ones that appear as a solid from a distance.

MATERIALS

1 fat quarter *each* of 2 assorted olive-green solids for blocks

1 fat quarter *each* of 3 assorted turquoise solids for blocks

1 fat quarter *each* of 2 different off-white solids for blocks

1 fat quarter *each* of 2 different dark-blue solids for blocks

1 fat quarter of light-gray solid for blocks

1 fat quarter of medium-tan solid for blocks

1 fat quarter of medium-blue solid for blocks

1⅓ yards of off-white solid for border

⅝ yard of fabric for binding

3¾ yards of fabric for backing

64" x 80" piece of batting

CUTTING

From *each* of the 12 fat quarters, cut:

1 square, 17" x 17" (12 total)

2 strips, 1½" x 18" or width of fat quarter (24 total)

cutting your fat quarters

Don't worry if you're not able to get an exact 17" square from each of your fat quarters. As long as they all begin the same size, you'll be fine. The quilt top will just be a tiny bit smaller.

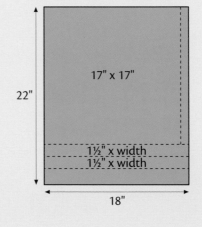

From the off-white solid for border, cut:

7 strips, 6" x 42"

From the fabric for binding, cut:

7 strips, 2½" x 42"

MAKING THE BLOCKS

Refer to "Stacking the Deck" on pages 9–12 for details as needed.

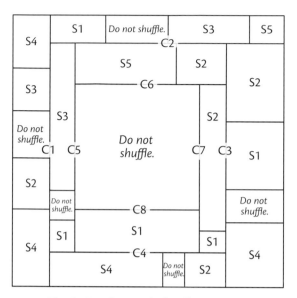

Block Cutting and Shuffling Guide
C = Cutting order
S = Shuffling order
Cut size: 17" x 17"

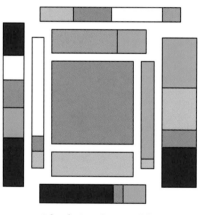

Block Sewing Guide

1. Arrange the 17" x 17" squares into two decks with six different squares in each deck.

2. Refer to the block cutting and shuffling guide above to free-form cut one deck using a straight ruler. As soon as you cut off one edge, slice it into sections as indicated in the guide and then move the pieces away from the stack so you don't accidentally cut into them again. Two of the sections will remain uncut. **Note:** Once the pieces are all sewn back together, the block will be cut

into wavy quarters, so plan ahead and try to keep most of your cuts out of the way of the exact vertical and horizontal center.

3. Shuffle the deck. The shuffling for this quilt is a lot of fun; there isn't a right or wrong way. You can refer to the block cutting and shuffling guide for one idea or switch it up as desired. I think it's fun to let the same colors touch, pairing up two different shapes. Leave your cut deck on your cutting mat, keeping it in its shuffled stack.

4. Refer to the block sewing guide at left to chain sew one section at a time of each stack. For example, sew all the pieces together for the first strip you cut from the original square. Use a small stitch length to prevent the seams from pulling apart later when sewing the quartered sections together. Press the seam allowances in one direction. When all of the pieces have been joined, replace the pieces in the block layout. Continue in this manner until all of the sections have been pieced, pressed, and replaced. Sew the sections together to make a total of six blocks. Keep the blocks together.

5. Repeat steps 2–4 to make the remaining six blocks.

6. Layer one block from each deck right sides up on your cutting surface. Cut each deck vertically and horizontally using the Creative Grids Split Seconds ruler, or cut the curves free-form by following the instructions in "Cutting Curves" on page 9. Be sure that the first and last 1" of the cutting line are both at a 90° angle to the square edges and that the intersecting lines are at a 90° angle to each other.

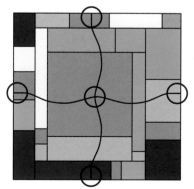

Cut the first and last 1" of the lines perpendicular to the edge of the block and make sure the intersecting lines are at a 90° angle to each other.

7. Shuffle the upper-right and lower-left sections to the bottom of the deck. Refer to "Sewing Curves" on page 11 to sew the upper sections together, and then sew the lower sections together. Press the seam allowances in opposite directions. Join the upper section to the lower section. Press the seam allowance in one direction. Trim the block to 14" x 14".

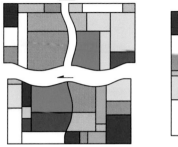
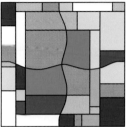

8. Repeat steps 6 and 7 to make a total of 12 blocks.

ASSEMBLING THE QUILT TOP

1. Refer to the quilt assembly diagram at right to arrange the blocks into four horizontal rows of three blocks each. Place a 1½" strip cut from the fat quarters on two sides of each block as shown. For each block, sew one strip to one side of the block. Press the seam allowances toward the strip. Trim the ends of the strip even with the sides of the block. Sew the remaining strip to the adjacent side of the block; trim the ends even with the sides of the block. Press the seam allowances toward the strip. Replace the block in the layout.

2. Pin and sew the blocks in each row together. Press the seam allowances in alternating directions from row to row. Sew the rows together. Press the seam allowances in one direction.

3. Referring to "Adding Borders" on page 8, sew the off-white 6"-wide border strips together end to end to make one long strip. Press the seam allowances open. Measure the length of the quilt top through the center and cut two border strips to this measurement. Pin and sew the borders to the sides of the quilt. Press the seam allowances toward the border strips. Measure the width of the quilt top through the center, including the borders just added, and cut two border strips to this measurement. Pin and sew the borders to the top and bottom of the quilt. Press the seam allowances toward the border strips.

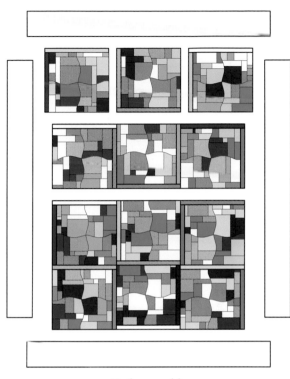

Quilt assembly

FINISHING YOUR QUILT

Refer to "Finishing the Quilt" on page 13 as needed.

1. Divide the backing crosswise into two equal panels, each approximately 64" long. Remove the selvages and sew the pieces together along a long edge to make a backing piece approximately 64" x 80"; press the seam allowance to one side.

2. Layer the quilt top with the batting and backing, keeping the backing seam parallel to the short edges of the quilt top. Baste the layers together using your favorite method.

3. Hand or machine quilt as desired.

4. Trim the backing and batting even with the edges of the quilt top and use the 2½"-wide strips to bind the quilt.

split seconds

The blocks in this quilt are simple to make and each one can be very different from the rest. I used a selection of warm and cool colors, but I'd also love to give this design a whirl with black and white fabrics.

Finished Quilt: 59¾" x 84½"

Finished Block: 13½" x 14"

Blocks Needed: 24

fabric tips

Choose two different colorways, and then select an equal number of light- and dark-value prints in each of those colorways. For my first colorway, I chose warm reds and golds. For my second, I chose cool greens, blues, and turquoise fabrics. Make sure to preview all your choices by using my 10-foot rule on page 7. The result is a quilt top with vertical waves, so try to picture what color you want your waves to read. Keep in mind, this technique could work with solid fabrics as well, or shake it up and use up your leftover blocks from other projects. Pair a pieced block with a solid fabric square the same size as your block, make a wave cut, and then sew them back together! I used fat quarters, but you could make the blocks with any size square.

MATERIALS

1 fat quarter *each* of 6 assorted gold batiks, 6 assorted red batiks, 6 assorted green and turquoise batiks, and 6 assorted dark-blue and dark-purple batiks for blocks and sashing

⅔ yard of fabric for binding

5¼ yards of fabric for backing

68" x 93" piece of batting

CUTTING

From *each* of the 6 assorted gold and 6 assorted red batiks, cut:

1 square, 17" x 17" (12 total)

1 strip, 2½" x 14½" (12 total)

From *each* of the 6 assorted green and turquoise and 6 assorted dark-blue and dark-purple batiks, cut:

1 square, 17" x 17" (12 total)

From the remainder of the assorted green, turquoise, dark-blue, and dark-purple batiks, cut a *total* of:

6 strips, 1¾" x 14½"

From the fabric for binding, cut:

8 strips, 2½" x 42"

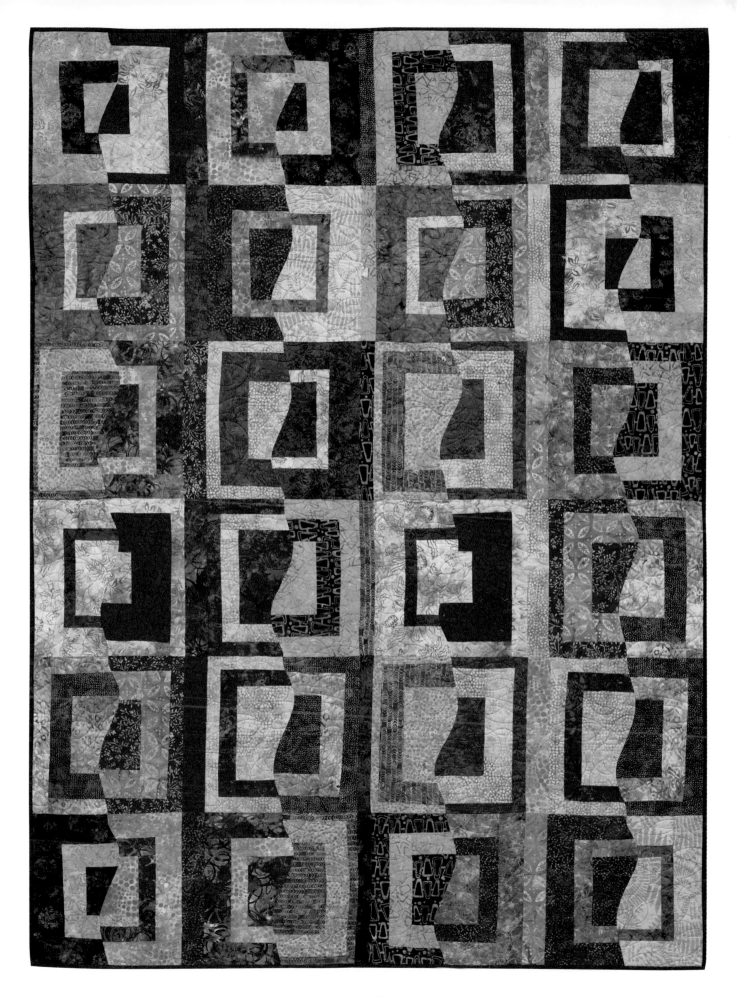

MAKING THE BLOCKS

Refer to "Stacking the Deck" on pages 9–12 for details as needed.

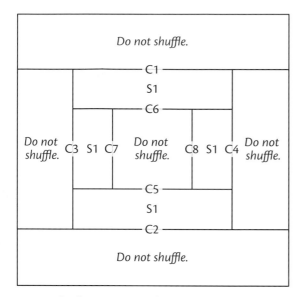

Block Cutting and Shuffling Guide
C = Cutting order
S = Shuffling order
Cut size: 17" x 17"

1. Arrange the 17" x 17" squares into six decks with one green/turquoise square and one dark-blue/dark-purple square in each deck, and six decks with one red square and one dark-purple square in each deck. Alternate the colors in each deck.

2. Refer to the block cutting and shuffling guide above to cut each deck using a straight ruler. Cut each deck slightly different.

3. Shuffle each deck as indicated on the block cutting and shuffling guide. Secure each shuffled deck to a piece of paper with a pin through all layers until you're ready to sew.

4. Sew the shuffled segments together in the exact opposite order they were cut. After you sew the first two pieces to the center square, trim the excess length of each newly added strip. Press the seam allowances away from the center square.

Make two blocks from each deck for a total of 24 blocks. Trim the blocks to 14½" x 14½".

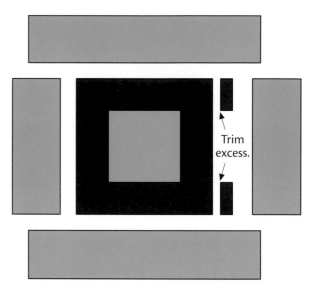

Trim excess.

5. Layer a gold-and-red block and a green/turquoise-and-blue/purple block right sides up on your cutting surface. Line up the edges as close as possible. Find the exact center of the blocks and make a wave cut using the Creative Grids Split Seconds ruler, or cut the curve free-form by following the instructions in "Cutting Curves" on page 9. Be sure that both the first and last 1" of the cutting line are at a 90° angle (or perpendicular to) the edge.

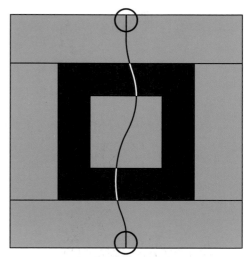

Cut the first and last 1" of the line perpendicular to the edge of the block.

6. Shuffle the top section of the right-hand side of the blocks to the bottom of the deck. Refer to "Sewing Curves" on page 11 to sew the sections of the top layer together, and then sew the sections of the bottom layer together to make two blocks. Press the seam allowances in one direction.

7. Repeat steps 5 and 6 with the remaining blocks.

ASSEMBLING THE QUILT TOP

1. Refer to the quilt assembly diagram below to arrange the blocks into six horizontal rows with four blocks in each row as shown. Insert the red and gold 2½" x 14½" sashing strips between the first and second blocks in each row and between the third and fourth blocks in each row. Insert the blue/purple 1¾" x 14½" strips between the second and third block in each row. Rearrange the blocks and sashing strips until you're satisfied with the layout.

2. Pin and sew the blocks in each row together. Press the seam allowances in alternating directions from row to row. Sew the rows together. Press the seam allowances in one direction.

FINISHING YOUR QUILT

Refer to "Finishing the Quilt" on page 13 as needed.

1. Divide the backing crosswise into two equal panels, each approximately 93" long. Remove the selvages and sew the pieces together along a long edge to make a backing piece approximately 80" x 93"; press the seam allowance to one side.

2. Layer the quilt top with the batting and backing, keeping the backing seam parallel to the long edges of the quilt top. Baste the layers together using your favorite method.

3. Hand or machine quilt as desired.

4. Trim the backing and batting even with the edges of the quilt top and use the 2½"-wide strips to bind the quilt.

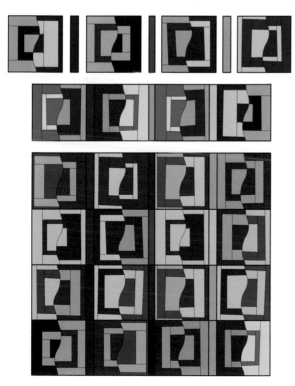

Quilt assembly

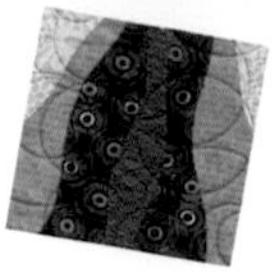

watermelon dreams

Two different units come together to create the Watermelon blocks in this quilt, with different colors winding vertically from the top to the bottom of each one. As with all the projects in this book, you can choose to cut wavy or straight lines.

Finished Quilt: 59½" x 81½"

Finished Block: 10" x 18"

Blocks Needed: 20

fabric tips

I chose a group of six different colors. Because the pieces in this quilt are sort of skinny and are mixed with so many different colors, it's important to choose prints that appear as solid from a distance.

MATERIALS

⅜ yard *each* of 3 assorted gray prints, 3 assorted yellowish-green prints, 3 assorted medium-blue prints, 3 assorted raspberry prints, 2 assorted turquoise prints, and 2 assorted medium-brown prints for blocks

1⅛ yards of medium-brown print for block frames

1⅛ yards of turquoise print for block frames

1⅛ yards of multicolored print for border

⅔ yard of fabric for binding

5 yards of fabric for backing

68" x 90" piece of batting

CUTTING

From the 16 prints for blocks, cut a *total* of:
36 rectangles, 9½" x 13"

From *each* of the medium-brown and turquoise prints, cut:
1 strip, 9½" x 42"; crosscut into 3 rectangles, 9½" x 13" (6 total)

17 strips, 1½" x 42"; crosscut into:

    20 strips, 1½" x 16½" (40 total)

    20 strips, 1½" x 10½" (40 total)

From the multicolored print, cut:
7 strips, 5" x 42"

From the fabric for binding, cut:
8 strips, 2½" x 42"

MAKING THE BLOCKS

Refer to "Stacking the Deck" on pages 9–12 for details as needed.

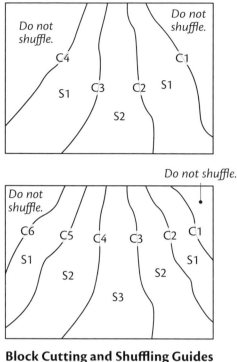

Block Cutting and Shuffling Guides
C = Cutting order
S = Shuffling order
Cut size: 9½" x 13"

1. Arrange the 9½" x 13" rectangles into seven decks with six different rectangles in each deck. Alternate contrasting prints.

2. Refer to the block cutting and shuffling guides above to cut each deck using the Creative Grids Curved Slotted ruler, or cut the curves free-form by following the instructions in "Cutting Curves" on page 9. Vary the position of the cuts in each deck, creating a "V" design, making either four or six cuts.

3. Shuffle each deck as indicated on the block cutting and shuffling guide. Secure each shuffled deck to a piece of paper with a pin through all layers until ready to sew.

4. Referring to "Sewing Curves" on page 11, sew the shuffled segments together to make six blocks from each deck for a total of 42 units. Try to keep the top edges flush as you sew. Keep in mind the edges will not be even along the bottom edge. Trim the units to 8½" x 8½".

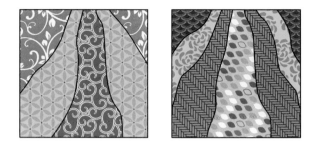

5. Sew two units together vertically, with the wide end of the strips meeting. Repeat to make a total of 20 pairs. You'll have two units left over. Sew the turquoise 1½" x 16½" strips to the sides of 10 pairs. Press the seam allowances toward the strips. Add the turquoise 1½" x 10½" strips to the top and bottom of these units to make 10 turquoise blocks. Press the seam allowances toward the strips. Repeat with the brown strips and remaining pairs to make 10 brown blocks.

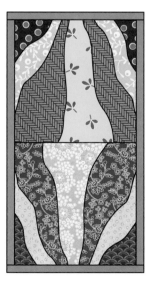
Make 10.

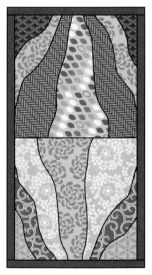
Make 10.

ASSEMBLING THE QUILT TOP

1. Refer to the quilt assembly diagram below to arrange the blocks into four horizontal rows of five blocks each, alternating the turquoise and brown blocks in each row and from row to row. Rearrange the blocks until you're satisfied with the layout.

2. Pin and sew the blocks in each row together. Press the seam allowance in alternating directions from row to row. Sew the rows together. Press the seam allowances in one direction.

3. Referring to "Adding Borders" on page 8, sew the multicolored print 5"-wide strips together end to end to make one long strip. Press the seam allowances open. Measure the length of the quilt top through the center and cut two border strips to this measurement. Pin and sew the borders to the sides of the quilt. Press the seam allowances toward the border strips. Measure the width of the quilt top through the center, including the borders just added, and cut two border strips to this measurement. Pin and sew the borders to the top and bottom of the quilt. Press the seam allowances toward the border strips.

FINISHING YOUR QUILT

Refer to "Finishing the Quilt" on page 13 as needed.

1. Divide the backing crosswise into two equal panels, each approximately 90" long. Remove the selvages and sew the pieces together along a long edge to make a backing piece approximately 80" x 90"; press the seam allowance to one side.

2. Layer the quilt top with the batting and backing, keeping the backing seam parallel to the long edges of the quilt top. Baste the layers together using your favorite method.

3. Hand or machine quilt as desired.

4. Trim the backing and batting even with the edges of the quilt top and use the 2½"-wide strips to bind the quilt.

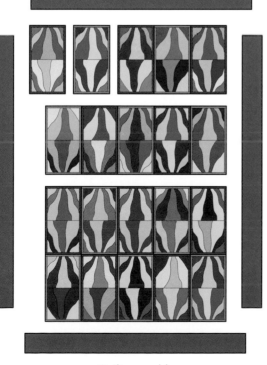

Quilt assembly

epicenter

The blocks in this quilt are very forgiving—after just a couple of skewed cuts, they're nicely squared. Each square is equivalent to one completed block, lending itself to smaller projects such as table runners or pillows.

Finished Quilt: 55½" x 77½"

Finished Block: 5½" x 5½"

Blocks Needed: 140

fabric tips

I used batiks for this quilt, but other fabrics will work just as well. I think fabrics that appear as solids from a distance work best. It's an easy stash quilt if you're willing to dive in and start cutting squares . . . 140 to be exact. You might notice a few more colors in my quilt than are listed; that's because I like to build my quilts a block or two at a time. So, if I feel like I need another color, I don't hesitate to cut a square or two to throw into the mix. The rule here is to cut the listed amount of lights, mediums, and darks. You can choose as many different colors as you like, as long as you stay within the light, medium, and dark range. If you want a larger quilt, the addition of a border always adds interest as well as size.

MATERIALS

¼ yard each of 4 assorted light-gold batiks for blocks

¼ yard each of 6 assorted medium-brown batiks for blocks

½ yard each of 7 assorted dark-brown batiks for blocks

⅝ yard of fabric for binding

4⅞ yards of fabric for backing

64" x 86" piece of batting

CUTTING

From each of the 4 assorted light-gold batiks, cut:
1 strip, 6½" x 42"; crosscut into 6 squares, 6½" x 6½" (24 total)

From each of the 6 assorted medium-brown batiks, cut:
1 strip, 6½" x 42"; crosscut into 6 squares, 6½" x 6½" (36 total)

From each of the 7 assorted dark-brown batiks, cut:
2 strips, 6½" x 42"; crosscut into 12 squares, 6½" x 6½" (84 total)

From the fabric for binding, cut:
7 strips, 2½" x 42"

MAKING THE BLOCKS

Refer to "Stacking the Deck" on pages 9–12 for details as needed.

1. Make the following decks, stacking a variety of 6½" x 6½" squares in the order listed:

   1 deck: dark, dark, dark, dark

   6 decks: dark, light, dark, medium

   8 decks: light, dark, light, dark

   10 decks: medium, dark, medium, dark

   10 decks: dark, dark, dark, medium

2. Work with one deck at a time and make sure the edges are all aligned. Use the Creative Grids Straight Out of Line ruler to mark the angled horizontal and vertical lines using the ruler marks for a 6½" square, or mark 2⅝" from each corner on the top square of each deck and use a straight ruler to cut the decks apart horizontally and vertically.

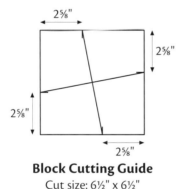

Block Cutting Guide
Cut size: 6½" x 6½"

3. Shuffle each deck as shown. Secure each shuffled deck to a piece of paper with a pin through all layers until you're ready to sew.

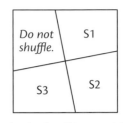

Block Shuffling Guide

4. Sew the blocks together one layer at a time. Sew the upper two pieces together, and then sew the bottom two pieces together. Press the seam allowances in alternate directions. Sew the top and bottom sections together, matching the center seam and referring to "Joining Angled Seams" on page 12. Press the seam allowances in one direction. Trim the blocks to 6" x 6". **Note:** It's OK if your blocks are larger or smaller as long as they're all the same size.

Make 4.

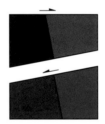

Make 40.   Make 40.

Make 24.   Make 32.

ASSEMBLING THE QUILT TOP

1. Refer to the quilt assembly diagram below to lay out the blocks in 14 horizontal rows of 10 blocks each. Rearrange the blocks until you're satisfied with the layout.

2. Pin and sew the blocks in each row together. Press the seam allowances in alternate directions from row to row. Sew the rows together. Press the seam allowances in one direction.

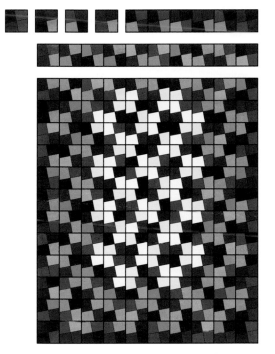

Quilt assembly

FINISHING YOUR QUILT

Refer to "Finishing the Quilt" on page 13 as needed.

1. Divide the backing crosswise into two equal panels, each approximately 86" long. Remove the selvages and sew the pieces together along a long edge to make a backing piece approximately 80" x 86"; press the seam allowance to one side.

2. Layer the quilt top with the batting and backing, keeping the backing seam parallel to the long edges of the quilt top. Baste the layers together using your favorite method.

3. Hand or machine quilt as desired.

4. Trim the backing and batting even with the edges of the quilt top and use the 2½"-wide strips to bind the quilt.

garden party

I have a fancy for birds lately. My mom always loved birds and I think I inherited this fascination from her. This little quilt is pretty quick to make and the birds can be positioned anywhere you like. You can add as many as you like too!

Finished Quilt: 44" x 68"

Finished Blocks: 7¼" x 7¼" and 7¼" x 8"

Blocks Needed: 36 center and 12 border

fabric tips

I chose a mix of colors that reminded me of trees and bright blue summer skies. The turquoise fabrics are all relatively the same value, whereas the browns range from lights to darks. The darks are used for the center blocks as well as in the pieced borders. The prints in each bring a few more colors to the party, both subtle and bold. I dove into my stash more than once, so if you see more different fabrics than the list calls for, that's why.

MATERIALS

½ yard *each* of 5 assorted brown prints ranging from light to dark for outer-border blocks

⅓ yard *each* of 6 assorted small-scale dark-brown prints for center blocks

⅓ yard *each* of 6 assorted turquoise prints for center blocks

¼ yard of black print for inner border

¼ yard of deep-red fabric for vine appliqués

7" x 9" rectangle *each* of 4 assorted black prints for bird appliqués

Scraps of assorted green prints for leaf appliqués

½ yard of fabric for binding

3 yards of fabric for backing

52" x 70" piece of batting

Freezer paper

2 yards of lightweight fusible web

CUTTING

From *each* of the 5 assorted turquoise prints, cut:
1 strip, 8½" x 42"; crosscut into 4 squares, 8½" x 8½" (20 total; you'll have 2 left over)

From *each* of the 5 assorted dark-brown prints, cut:
1 strip, 8½" x 42"; crosscut into 4 squares, 8½" x 8½" (20 total; you'll have 2 left over)

From *each* of the 5 assorted light- to dark-brown prints, cut:
1 strip, 9" x 42"; crosscut into 3 rectangles, 9" x 13" (15 total)
1 strip, 4" x 42"; crosscut into 3 rectangles, 4" x 7¾" (15 total)

From the black print, cut:
3 strips, 1" x 42"

From the fabric for binding, cut:
6 strips, 2½" x 42"

MAKING THE CENTER BLOCKS

Refer to "Shuffling the Deck" on pages 9–12 for details as needed.

1. Arrange the 8½" x 8½" squares into three decks with three blue squares and three dark-brown squares in each deck. Alternate the blue and brown squares in each deck.

2. You have three options for cutting the decks apart.

   Option 1: Use the Creative Grids Straight Out of Line ruler to mark the angled horizontal and vertical lines using the ruler marks for an 8½" square.

   Option 2: On the top square of each deck, make a mark 3½" from both sides of the lower-left and upper-right corners. Using a straight ruler, cut the decks horizontally and vertically from mark to mark as shown.

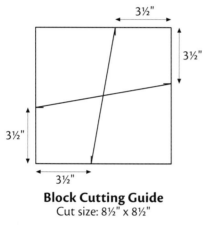

Block Cutting Guide
Cut size: 8½" x 8½"

Option 3: Cut two 3½" x 3½" squares from the freezer paper. With the shiny side down, press a square in opposite corners of the top square on one of the decks. Cut from corner to corner as shown.

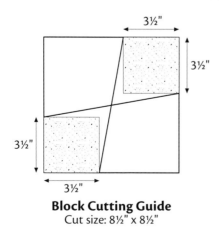

Block Cutting Guide
Cut size: 8½" x 8½"

3. Shuffle each deck as shown. Secure each shuffled deck to a piece of paper with a pin through all layers until you're ready to sew.

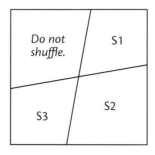

Block Shuffling Guide

4. Sew the blocks together one layer at a time. Sew the upper two pieces together, and then sew the lower two pieces together. Press the seam allowances in alternate directions. Sew the top and bottom sections together, matching the center seam and referring to "Joining Angled Seams" on page 12. Press the seam allowances in one direction. Trim the blocks to 7¾" x 7¾". **Note:** It's OK if your blocks are larger or smaller as long as they're all the same size. Just make sure the border blocks are also trimmed to the same width.

MAKING THE BORDER BLOCKS

Refer to "Shuffling the Deck" on pages 9–12 for details as needed.

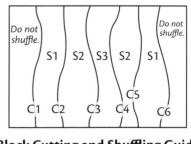

Block Cutting and Shuffling Guide
C = Cutting order
S = Shuffling order
Cut size: 9"x 13"

1. Arrange the 9" x 13" rectangles into two decks of six rectangles each, alternating the values in each deck. Each deck will have one duplicate fabric. You'll have three rectangles left over.

2. Refer to the block cutting and shuffling guide on page 74 to cut each deck using the Creative Grids Curved Slotted ruler, or cut the curves free-form by following the instructions in "Cutting Curves" on page 9. Cut each deck differently, varying the position of the cuts.

3. Shuffle each deck as indicated on the block cutting and shuffling guide. Secure each shuffled deck to a piece of paper with a pin through all layers until you're ready to sew.

4. Referring to "Sewing Curves" on page 11, sew the shuffled segments together to make six blocks from each deck for a total of 12 blocks. Press the seam allowances in one direction. Trim each block to 8½" x 7¾".

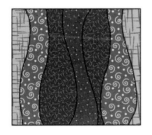

ASSEMBLING THE QUILT TOP

1. Refer to the quilt assembly diagram at right to arrange the center blocks into six rows of six blocks each, making sure the brown portions of each block are in the upper-left and lower-right corners. Rearrange the blocks until you're satisfied with the layout.

2. Pin and sew the blocks in each row together. Press the seam allowances in alternating directions from row to row. Sew the rows together. Press the seam allowances in one direction.

3. Refer to "Adding Borders" on page 8 and the quilt assembly diagram to sew the 1"-wide black print strips together end to end. Measure the width of the quilt top through the center and cut two inner-border strips to this length. Sew the strips to the top and bottom of the quilt top. Press the seam allowances toward the border strips.

4. Refer to the assembly diagram to sew an assorted brown 4" x 7¾" rectangle to one short end of each of the pieced border blocks. Press the seam allowances toward the rectangles. You'll have three rectangles left over.

5. Refer to the assembly diagram to sew six border blocks from step 4 together along the long edges, alternating the position of the brown rectangle from top to bottom. Press the seam allowances in one direction. Repeat to make a total of two outer-border strips. The strips should measure 44" long.

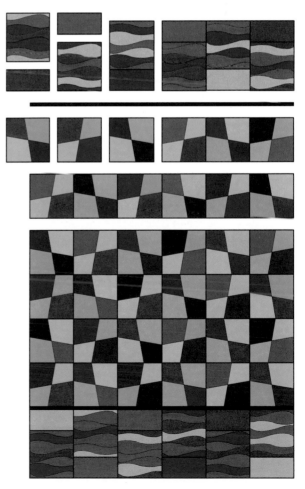

Quilt assembly

6. Refer to "Fusible-Web Appliqué" on page 7 and use the patterns on page 77 to trace the shapes for the outer-border appliqués onto fusible web. You can make any arrangement that you like or refer to the photo on page 73. I like to work as I go. The vine was elongated to span the length of the strip, but you could make several shorter vines if desired, or use more or fewer birds and leaves. Once you've traced the desired shapes onto the fusible web, cut out the center of the fusible web inside each shape, leaving approximately 1" for fusing. Follow the manufacturer's instructions to apply the fusible-web shapes to the desired scraps of fabric, and then cut them out on the marked lines.

7. Arrange the appliqués on the outer-border strips as desired. When you're happy with your arrangement, fuse and then stitch the appliqués in place. I stitched my shapes about ⅛" inside the edge. I also like to do what I call "sketch appliqué." To do this, I use my darning foot and "sketch" over the bird and leaf shapes using the thread in my needle as I would the lead in a pencil.

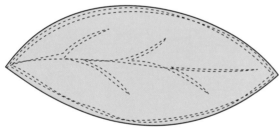

8. Sew the appliquéd outer-border strips to the top and bottom of the quilt top. Press the seam allowances toward the inner border.

FINISHING YOUR QUILT

Refer to "Finishing the Quilt" on page 13 as needed.

1. Divide the backing crosswise into two equal panels, each approximately 52" long. Remove the selvages and sew the pieces together along a long edge to make a backing piece approximately 52" x 80"; press the seam allowance to one side.

2. Layer the quilt top with the batting and backing, keeping the backing seam parallel to the short edges of the quilt top. Baste the layers together using your favorite method.

3. Hand or machine quilt as desired.

4. Trim the backing and batting even with the edges of the quilt top and use the 2½"-wide strips to bind the quilt.

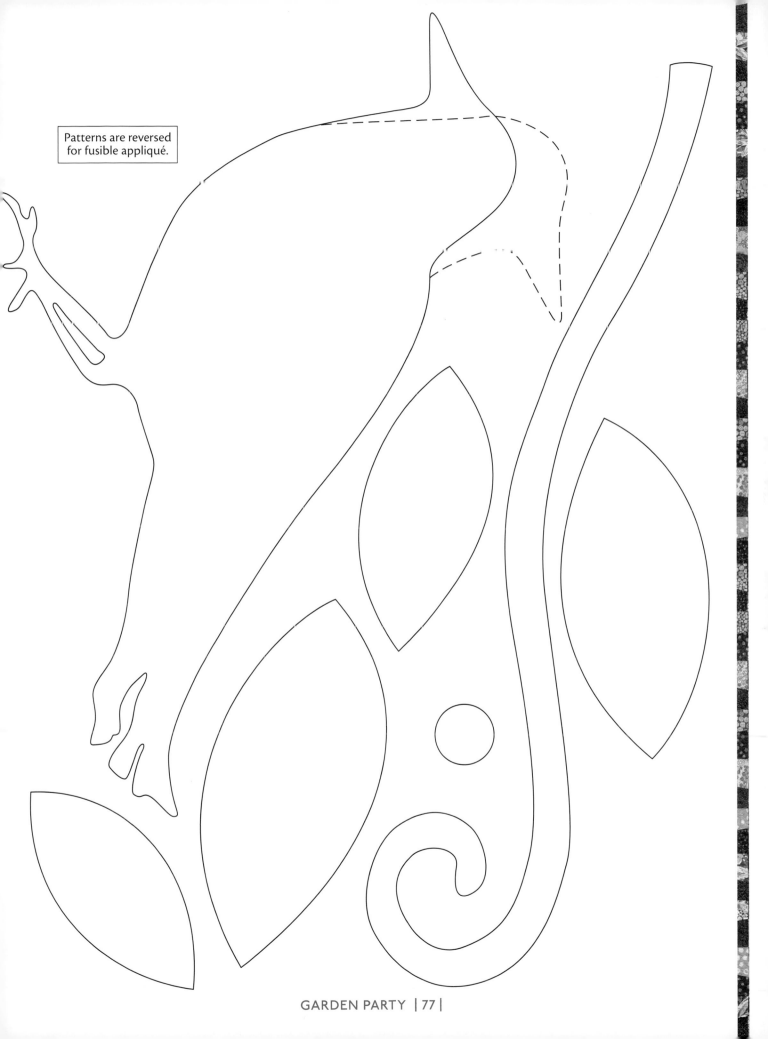

Patterns are reversed
for fusible appliqué.

good vibrations

This design uses a block I call No Match Patch for the light areas of the quilt. The block will always shrink 1", regardless of what size square or rectangle you begin with. There isn't a right or wrong way to shuffle, and there are no seams to match! Pairing it up with wavy half-square triangles doubles the number of blocks and creates a scrappy appearance that could be laid out in a variety of ways.

Finished Quilt: 67½" x 85½"

Finished Block: 9" x 9"

Blocks Needed: 48

fabric tips

You could really shake up things in this design with different fabric choices. Begin by choosing the fabrics for your No Match Patch block. Choose a variety of four light prints with a white or light background. Choose four more dark, small-scale prints to go with the light. I picked blue and turquoise. In retrospect, I could have used a bit darker mix. The final selection is for the Half-Square-Triangle blocks. I chose a mix of six different medium to dark blue and purple prints that don't have any light spots in the background.

MATERIALS

⅓ yard *each* of 4 assorted light prints for No Match Patch blocks

⅓ yard *each* of 4 assorted medium-blue and turquoise prints for No Match Patch blocks

⅓ yard *each* of 6 assorted medium-to-dark-blue, turquoise, and purple prints for Half-Square-Triangle blocks

1¾ yards of dark-purple print for border

⅔ yard of fabric for binding

5¼ yards of fabric for backing

76" x 94" piece of batting

CUTTING

From *each* of the 4 assorted light prints, cut:
1 strip, 11" x 42"; crosscut into 3 squares, 11" x 11" (12 total)

From *each* of the 4 medium-blue and turquoise prints, cut:
1 strip, 11" x 42"; crosscut into 3 squares, 11" x 11" (12 total)

From *each* of the 6 medium-to-dark-blue, turquoise, and purple prints, cut:
1 strip, 10" x 42"; crosscut into 4 squares, 10" x 10" (24 total)

From the dark-purple print, cut:
8 strips, 7" x 42"

From the fabric for binding, cut:
8 strips, 2½" x 42"

MAKING THE NO MATCH PATCH BLOCKS

Refer to "Shuffling the Deck" on pages 9–12 for details as needed.

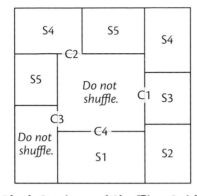

Block Cutting and Shuffling Guide
C = Cutting order
S = Shuffling order
Cut size: 11" x 11"

1. Arrange the 11" x 11" squares into two decks of three different light squares and three different medium squares in each deck. Alternate the light and medium squares in each deck.

2. Refer to the block cutting and shuffling guide above to cut each deck using a straight ruler. Cut each deck slightly different. As soon as you cut off the first piece, slice it into sections as indicated in the guide and then move the pieces away from the stack so you don't accidentally cut into them again. Two of the sections will remain uncut.

3. Shuffle each deck. The block cutting and shuffling guide gives you one option, but there is no right or wrong way to shuffle the decks. Secure each shuffled deck to a piece of paper with a pin through all layers until you're ready to sew.

4. Sew the pieces for each section together, and then sew the sections together to make a total of 24 blocks. Trim the blocks to 10" x 10".

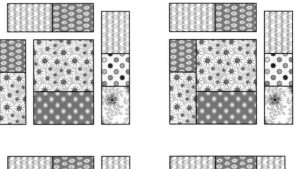

MAKING THE GOOD VIBRATIONS BLOCKS

Refer to "Shuffling the Deck" on pages 9–12 for details as needed.

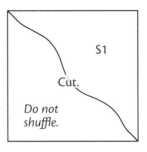

Block Cutting and Shuffling Guide
S = Shuffling order
Cut size: 10" x 10"

1. Arrange the 10" x 10" squares and the No Match Patch blocks into 24 decks with one square and one block in each deck.

2. Referring to the block cutting and shuffling guide above, cut each deck in half diagonally using the Creative Grids Curves for Squares ruler, or cut the curves free-form by following the instructions in "Cutting Curves" on page 9. Be sure that the first and last 1" of the cutting line are both at a 45° angle to the square edges.

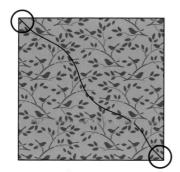

Cut the first and last 1"
of the diagonal line at a 45° angle.

3. Shuffle each deck as indicated on the block cutting and shuffling guide. Secure each shuffled deck to a piece of paper with a pin through all layers until you're ready to sew.

4. Referring to "Sewing Curves" on page 11, sew the shuffled segments together to make two blocks from each deck for a total of 48 blocks. Press the seam allowances toward the unpieced half. Trim each block to 9½" x 9½".

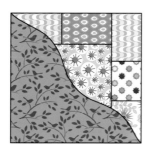

ASSEMBLING THE QUILT TOP

1. Refer to the quilt assembly diagram at right to arrange the blocks into eight horizontal rows of six blocks each, rotating the blocks to create the design. Rearrange the blocks until you're satisfied with the layout.

2. Pin and sew the blocks in each row together. Press the seam allowances in alternating directions from row to row. Sew the rows together. Press the seam allowances in one direction.

3. Referring to "Adding Borders" on page 8, sew the 7"-wide purple strips together end to end to make one long strip. Press the seam allowances open. Measure the length of the quilt top through the center and cut two border strips to this measurement. Pin and sew the borders to the sides

of the quilt. Press the seam allowances toward the border strips. Measure the width of the quilt top through the center, including the borders just added, and cut two border strips to this measurement. Pin and sew the borders to the top and bottom of the quilt. Press the seam allowances toward the border strips.

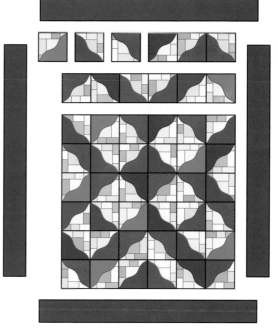

Quilt assembly

FINISHING YOUR QUILT

Refer to "Finishing the Quilt" on page 13 as needed.

1. Divide the backing crosswise into two equal panels, each approximately 94" long. Remove the selvages and sew the pieces together along a long edge to make a backing piece approximately 80" x 94"; press the seam allowance to one side.

2. Layer the quilt top with the batting and backing, keeping the backing seam parallel to the long edges of the quilt top. Baste the layers together using your favorite method.

3. Hand or machine quilt as desired.

4. Trim the backing and batting even with the edges of the quilt top and use the 2½"-wide strips to bind the quilt.

swish

Create an optical illusion with Hourglass blocks that appear to be wavy squares. Side setting triangles finish the design and border the quilt top.

Finished Quilt: 57⅜" x 80⅛"

Finished Block: 8" x 8"

Blocks Needed: 38 Hourglass and 20 Edge

fabric tips

I chose six light prints in shades of beige and gray for the light part of the block. Make sure these prints are mostly small scale, almost appearing as a solid from a distance. The dark fabrics for the blocks are a mix of medium-scale multicolored prints.

MATERIALS

⅓ yard *each* of 6 assorted small-scale light beige and gray prints

⅓ yard *each* of 6 assorted medium-scale dark blue, brown, and red prints

1⅞ yards of dark-red print for setting triangles

⅔ yard of fabric for binding

5 yards of fabric for backing

68" x 90" piece of batting

CUTTING

From *each* of the 6 assorted light prints, cut:
1 strip, 9½" x 42"; crosscut into 4 squares, 9½" x 9½" (24 total). Cut each square in half diagonally to make 8 triangles (48 total).

From *each* of the 6 assorted dark prints, cut:
1 strip, 9½" x 42"; crosscut into 4 squares, 9½" x 9½" (24 total). Cut each square in half diagonally to make 8 triangles (48 total).

From the dark-red print, cut:
3 strips, 13½" x 42"; crosscut into:

   6 squares, 13½" x 13½"; cut each square into quarters diagonally to yield 24 side setting triangles

   2 squares, 9" x 9"

2 strips, 9" x 42"; crosscut into 8 squares, 9" x 9"

From the fabric for binding, cut:
8 strips, 2½" x 42"

MAKING THE HOURGLASS BLOCKS

Refer to "Shuffling the Deck" on pages 9–12 for details as needed.

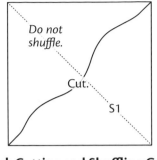

Block Cutting and Shuffling Guide
S = Shuffling order
Cut size: 9½" x 9½"

1. Sew each light triangle to a dark triangle along the long edges to make 48 half-square-triangle units. Trim each unit to 9" x 9".

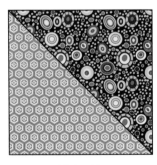

Make 48.

2. Set aside 10 of the half-square-triangle units for the Edge blocks. Arrange the remaining 38 units into 19 decks with two units in each deck. Alternate the position of the light and dark halves in each deck.

3. Referring to the block cutting and shuffling guide at left, cut each deck in half diagonally in the opposite direction as the seams of the half-square-triangle units using the Creative Grids Curves for Squares ruler, or cut the curves free-form by following the instructions in "Cutting Curves" on page 9. Be sure that the first and last 1" of the cutting line are both at a 45° angle to the square edges.

Cut the first and last 1"
of the diagonal line at a 45° angle.

4. Shuffle each deck as indicated in the block cutting and shuffling guide. Secure each shuffled deck to a piece of paper with a pin through all layers until you're ready to sew.

5. Referring to "Sewing Curves" on page 11, sew the shuffled segments together to make two blocks from each deck for a total of 38 blocks. Press the seam allowances in one direction. Trim the blocks to 8½" x 8½".

MAKING THE EDGE BLOCKS

Refer to "Shuffling the Deck" on pages 9–12 for details as needed.

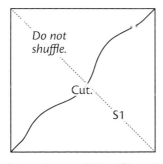

Block Cutting and Shuffling Guide
S = Shuffling order
Cut size: 9" x 9"

1. Arrange the remaining 10 half-square-triangle units and dark red 9" x 9" squares into 10 decks with one half-square-triangle unit and one square in each deck.

2. Referring to the block cutting and shuffling guide above, cut eight of the decks in half diagonally in the opposite direction as the seams of the half-square-triangle units using the Creative Grids Curves for Rectangles ruler, or cut the curves free-form by following the instructions in "Cutting Curves" on page 9. Be sure that the first and last 1" of the cutting line are both at a 45° angle to the square edges. Set the remaining two decks aside.

3. Shuffle each deck as indicated on the block cutting and shuffling guide. Secure each shuffled deck to a piece of paper with a pin through all layers until you're ready to sew.

4. Referring to "Sewing Curves" on page 11, sew the shuffled segments together to make one A block and one B block from each deck for a total of eight A blocks and eight B blocks.

Block A

Block B

5. Cut the remaining two decks in half diagonally in the same manner as the decks in step 2 using a straight ruler. Shuffle the decks as described in step 3. Refer to step 4 to sew the B blocks from each deck together. Unsew the pieced half of the remaining two blocks and reverse the position of the triangles. Sew the triangles back together and then sew the pieced units to the red half of the block to complete two additional B blocks. You'll now have a total of eight A blocks and 12 B blocks.

Unsew.

Reverse triangles.

Block B.
Make 2.

6. Trim each block to 8½" x 8½".

ASSEMBLING THE QUILT TOP

1. Refer to the quilt assembly diagram below to arrange the Hourglass and Edge blocks and the setting triangles into diagonal rows. Rearrange the blocks until you're satisfied with the layout.

2. Pin and sew the blocks and setting triangles in each row together. Press the seam allowances in alternating directions from row to row. Sew the rows together, adding the joined corner triangles last. Press the seam allowances in one direction. The setting triangles were cut oversized, so you'll need to trim the quilt-top edges a minimum of ¼" from the block points, keeping the distance consistant on each side.

Quilt assembly

FINISHING YOUR QUILT

Refer to "Finishing the Quilt" on page 13 as needed.

1. Divide the backing crosswise into two equal panels, each approximately 90" long. Remove the selvages and sew the pieces together along a long edge to make a backing piece approximately 80" x 90"; press the seam allowance to one side.

2. Layer the quilt top with the batting and backing, keeping the backing seam parallel to the long edges of the quilt top. Baste the layers together using your favorite method.

3. Hand or machine quilt as desired.

4. Trim the backing and batting even with the edges of the quilt top and use the 2½"-wide strips to bind the quilt.

well connected

This quilt might look like it involves a lot of cutting, but it's really a breeze to make. The blocks are all interconnected, floating on a colorful background. You could easily incorporate T-shirt logos or photo transfers in place of some of the squares. Use your imagination to see what you come up with!

Finished Quilt: 54½" x 74½"

Finished Blocks: 10" x 10" and 7" x 10"

Blocks Needed: 24 Well Connected and 24 Border

fabric tips

Choose a variety of multicolored light- to medium-value prints for the background. Make sure they blend somewhat when you look at them from a distance and that they look good together. For the squares, choose a variety of dark blue and purple prints. It's OK to use large-scale prints, but stay away from any prints with a white background if you really want your squares to stand out.

MATERIALS

⅞ yard *each* of 5 assorted dark-value prints for blocks

¾ yard *each* of 4 assorted light- to medium-value multicolored prints for background

⅝ yard of fabric for binding

4½ yards of fabric for backing

63" x 83" piece of batting

CUTTING

From the 4 assorted light- to medium-value multicolored prints, cut a *total* of:

10 rectangles, 8" x 11"

2 strips, 7¾" x 13" (cut from 2 different fabrics)

4 strips, 6¾" x 13" (cut from 4 different fabrics)

2 strips, 5¾" x 13" (cut from 2 different fabrics)

4 squares, 4½" x 4½"

4 rectangles, 2¾" x 6"

12 squares, 2¾" x 2¾"

4 rectangles, 2¼" x 7"

20 squares, 2¼" x 2¼"

2 rectangles, 1¾" x 8"

16 squares, 1¾" x 1¾"

From the 5 assorted dark-value prints, cut a *total* of:

12 squares, 10½" x 10½"

10 rectangles, 8" x 11"

4 squares, 8" x 8"

5 squares, 7" x 7"

3 squares, 6" x 6"

12 squares, 4½" x 4½"

8 strips, 1¼" x 13"

From the fabric for binding, cut:

7 strips, 2½" x 42"

MAKING THE WELL CONNECTED BLOCKS

Refer to "Shuffling the Deck" on pages 9–12 for details as needed.

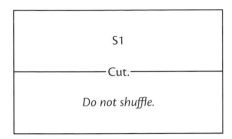

Block Cutting and Shuffling Guide
S = Shuffling order

1. Arrange the 7¾" x 13" strips into one deck (mark this deck A), the 6¾" x 13" strips into two decks with two strips in each deck (mark these decks B), and the 5¾" x 13" strips into one deck (mark this deck C).

2. Refer to the block cutting and shuffling guide to cut each deck in half lengthwise using a straight ruler. **Note:** To easily find the center, fold the long edges of the rectangles together and make a crease in the fold.

3. Shuffle each deck as indicated on the block cutting and shuffling guide.

4. Sew a dark 1¼" x 13" strip between the strips of each deck. Press the seam allowances toward the dark fabric. Crosscut the strips in each deck into the amount of segments shown.

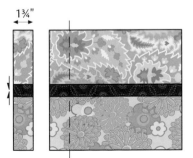

Deck A.
Make 2. Cut 14 segments.

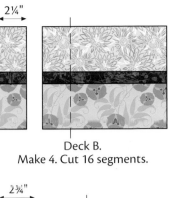

Deck B.
Make 4. Cut 16 segments.

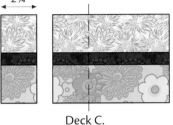

Deck C.
Make 2. Cut 8 segments.

5. Using the four dark 8" squares, the deck A segments from step 4, the light 1¾" squares, and the light 1¾" x 8" rectangles, make the following A blocks.

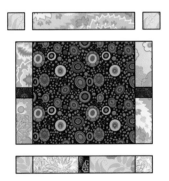

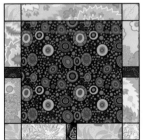

Make 2.

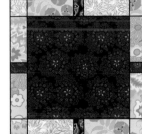

Make 2.

A blocks

6. Using the five dark 7" squares, the deck B segments from step 4, the light 2¼" squares, and the light 2¼" x 7" rectangles, make the following B blocks in the same manner as the A blocks.

Make 1.

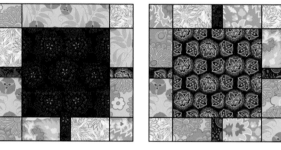

Make 2.   Make 2.

B blocks

7. Using the three dark 6" squares, the deck C segments from step 4, the light 2¾" squares, and the light 2¾" x 6" rectangles, make the following C blocks in the same manner as the A and B blocks.

Make 1.   Make 2.

C blocks

MAKING THE BORDER BLOCKS

Refer to "Shuffling the Deck" on pages 9–12 for details as needed.

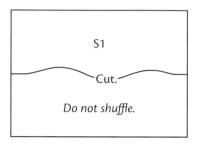

S1

Cut.

Do not shuffle.

Border Block Cutting and Shuffling Guide
S = Shuffling order
Cut size: 8" x 11"

1. Arrange the 8" x 11" rectangles into five decks with two different light rectangles and two different dark rectangles in each deck. Alternate the light and dark rectangles in each deck.

2. Refer to the block cutting and shuffling guide above to cut each deck using the Creative Grids Split Seconds ruler, or cut the curves free-form by following the instructions in "Cutting Curves" on page 9. Be sure that the first and last 1" of the cutting line is at a 90° angle to the rectangle edges.

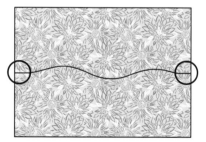

Cut through the exact center, cutting the first and last 1" perpendicular to the edge of the rectangle.

3. Shuffle each deck as indicated on the block cutting and shuffling guide. Secure each shuffled deck to a piece of paper with a pin through all layers until ready to sew.

4. Referring to "Sewing Curves" on page 11, sew the shuffled segments together to make four blocks from each deck for a total of 20 blocks. Press the seam allowances toward the dark fabric. Trim the blocks to 10½" long. It doesn't matter how wide they're as long as they're all the same size and you keep the seam centered on each block.

5. Arrange three dark 4½" squares and one light 4½" square into two rows of two squares each. Sew the squares in each row together. Press the seam allowances in alternate directions. Sew the rows together. Press the seam allowances toward the light half. Repeat to make a total of four corner units. Trim the units to the same width as the border blocks, keeping the seams centered.

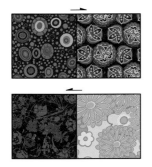
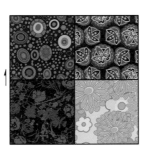

Make 4.

ASSEMBLING THE QUILT TOP

1. Refer to the quilt assembly diagram at right to arrange the Well Connected blocks, the dark 10½" squares, the Border blocks, and the border corner units into eight horizontal rows as shown. You can rearrange the blocks if desired, but make sure all the "pins" of the A, B, and C blocks are arranged so they connect to a 10½" square and don't point out toward the border.

2. Sew the pieces in each horizontal row together, including the border sections. Press the seam allowances in alternating directions from row to row. Sew the rows together. Press the seam allowances in one direction.

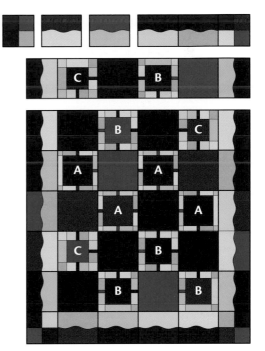

Quilt assembly

FINISHING YOUR QUILT

Refer to "Finishing the Quilt" on page 13 as needed.

1. Divide the backing crosswise into two equal panels, each approximately 83" long. Remove the selvages and sew the pieces together along a long edge to make a backing piece approximately 80" x 83"; press the seam allowance to one side.

2. Layer the quilt top with the batting and backing, keeping the backing seam parallel to the long edges of the quilt top. Baste the layers together using your favorite method.

3. Hand or machine quilt as desired.

4. Trim the backing and batting even with the edges of the quilt top and use the 2½"-wide strips to bind the quilt.

urban sprawl

I predict that you'll find it easy to get carried away with this project. Every block is the equivalent of one square of fabric and is perfect for my No Match Patch technique. With this quilt, I used the method with skewed cuts in two different sizes, and then floated the blocks to the edges of the quilt and mixed them in with the border.

Finished Quilt: 60½" x 83"

Finished Blocks: 3¾" x 3¾" and 7½" x 7½"

Blocks Needed: 72 small and 48 large

fabric tips

Batiks work great with this design. There are a lot of small pieces, but the tone-on-tone batiks make each piece stand out. I chose to work with earthy colors in shades of green, gold, beige, and brown, and then I threw in a little bit of teal to make things pop. Half of my prints are medium to light and the remaining half are dark. I chose a green border with hints of blue to pull it all together.

MATERIALS

½ yard *each* of 6 assorted light- to medium-value tone-on-tone batiks in gold, beige, gray, and light brown

½ yard *each* of 6 assorted medium- to dark-value tone-on-tone batiks in steel gray, rust, dark brown, and teal

1⅓ yards of fabric for border

⅔ yard of fabric for binding

5⅛ yards of fabric for backing

67" x 90" piece of batting

CUTTING

From *each* of the 12 batiks, cut:
1 strip, 9½" x 42"; crosscut into 4 squares, 9½" x 9½" (48 total)

1 strip, 6" x 42"; crosscut into 6 squares, 6" x 6" (72 total)

From the remainder of the batiks, cut a *total* of:
2 squares, 4¼" x 4¼"

From the fabric for binding, cut:
8 strips, 2½" x 42"

MAKING THE URBAN SPRAWL BLOCKS

Refer to "Shuffling the Deck" on pages 9–12 for details as needed.

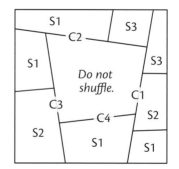

Block Cutting and Shuffling Guide
C = Cutting order
S = Shuffling order
Cut size: Large, 9½" x 9½"; Small, 6" x 6"

1. Arrange the 9½" x 9½" squares into eight decks with three different light to medium squares and three different medium to dark squares in each deck. Alternate the light and dark squares in each deck.

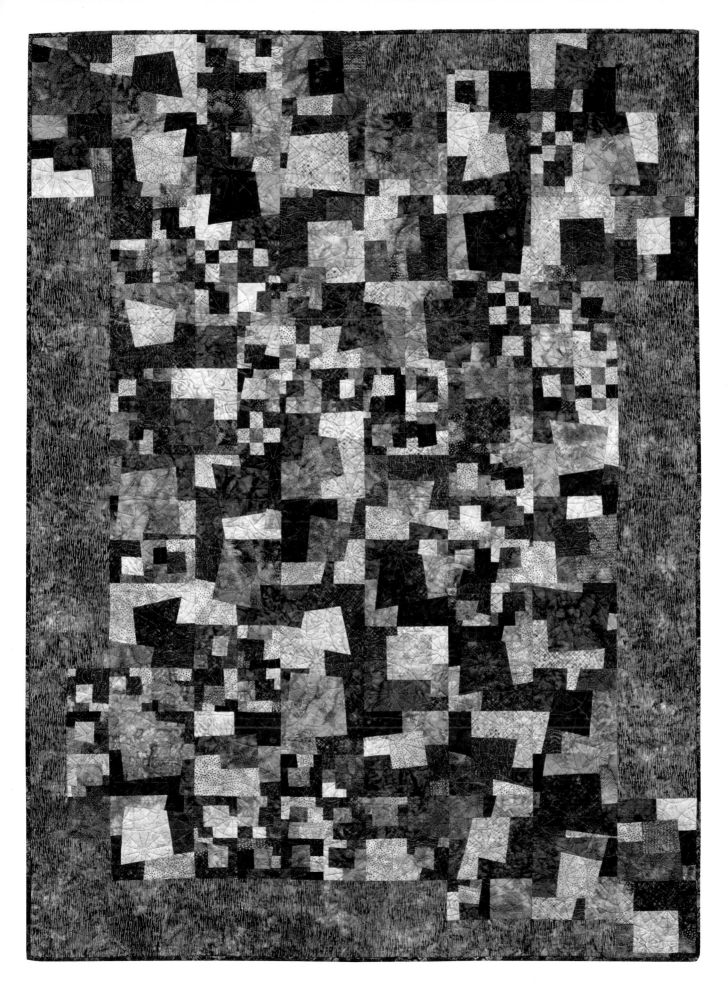

2. Refer to the block cutting and shuffling guide on page 92 to free-form cut each deck using a straight ruler. Cut each deck slightly different. I made a few skewed cuts, but you could make simple straight cuts if you prefer. As soon as you cut off one edge, slice it into sections as indicated on the guide and then move the pieces away from the stack so you don't accidentally cut into them again. Two of the sections will remain uncut.

3. Shuffle each deck as indicated on the block cutting and shuffling guide. It's okay to shuffle the deck differently than the way I did. Secure each shuffled deck to a piece of paper with a pin through all layers until you're ready to sew.

4. Sew the shuffled pieces for each section together, and then sew the sections together to make a total of 48 large blocks. Trim the blocks to 8" x 8".

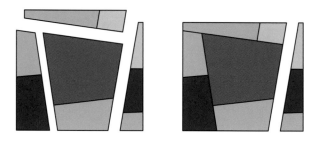

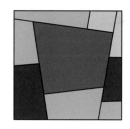

5. Arrange the 6" x 6" squares into 10 decks of three different light to medium squares and three different medium to dark squares in each deck. Alternate the light and dark squares in each deck. Repeat steps 2–4 to make a total of 60 small blocks. Trim the blocks to 4¼" x 4¼".

MAKING THE NINE PATCH BLOCKS

Refer to "Shuffling the Deck" on pages 9–12 for details as needed.

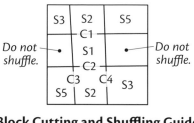

Block Cutting and Shuffling Guide
C = Cutting order
S = Shuffling order
Cut size: 6" x 6"

1. From six of the remaining 6" squares, make one deck with three different light to medium squares and three different medium to dark squares. Alternate the light and dark squares in the deck. Trim the remaining six batik 6" squares to 4¼" x 4¼" and set them aside until you're ready to assemble the quilt.

2. Refer to the block cutting and shuffling guide above to free-form cut the deck using a straight ruler.

3. Shuffle the deck as indicated on the block cutting and shuffling guide.

4. Sew the shuffled pieces for each block together to make a total of six Nine Patch blocks. Trim the blocks to 4¼" x 4¼".

ASSEMBLING THE QUILT TOP

1. Refer to the quilt assembly diagram below as a loose starting point for laying out the blocks in sections. The length and width of the sections can be changed, as long as the sections can be combined into vertical rows. Keep the following in mind: The length of the quilt top is equal to 8" square blocks; the width is equal to eight large blocks. Two 4¼" square blocks or squares equal the width and length of one large block.

2. Once you're pleased with the arrangement, join the blocks in each section. To fill in along the edges, cut 8"-wide pieces from the border fabric to equal the length of the joined block pieces plus ½" for seam allowance. Try to always have seams opposing one another. If this isn't possible, refer to "Flippers" on page 12. Sew the sections into vertical rows. Press the seam allowances in alternating directions from row to row. Sew the rows together. Press the seam allowance in one direction.

FINISHING YOUR QUILT

Refer to "Finishing the Quilt" on page 13 as needed.

1. Divide the backing crosswise into two equal panels, each approximately 90" long. Remove the selvages and sew the pieces together along a long edge to make a backing piece approximately 80" x 92"; press the seam allowance to one side.

2. Layer the quilt top with the batting and backing, keeping the backing seam parallel to the long edges of the quilt top. Baste the layers together using your favorite method.

3. Hand or machine quilt as desired.

4. Trim the backing and batting even with the edges of the quilt top and use the 2½"-wide strips to bind the quilt.

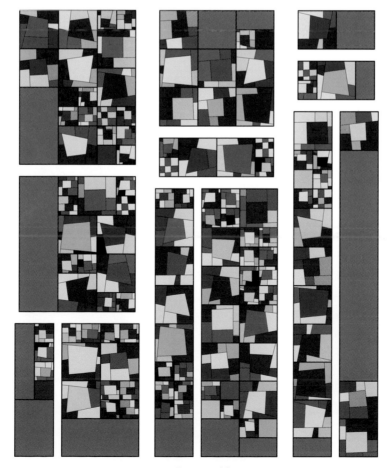

Quilt assembly

about the author

Karla Alexander has enjoyed making quilts for many years, and has been passionately designing them for more than 15 years. She got her start in sewing as a young girl, watching over her mother's shoulder as she sewed for her job. Karla remembers her mother frequently returning to the sewing room after she was done working to make quilts or to make clothing for Karla and her four siblings. These memories eventually inspired Karla to take off in her own direction with fabric—designing quilts; creating her own business, Saginaw Street Quilt Company; and designing a line of rulers for Creative Grids that work well with many of her books and patterns.

This is Karla's seventh book on the art of quiltmaking. Her philosophy regarding quilting is to enjoy the process, learn from your experiences, and take what you learn from one project to the next. As a teacher, she encourages her students to separate themselves from the mainstream and develop their own quilting identity by putting a spin on whatever style or technique catches their fancy. "You may not know the exact outcome of what you're doing but at least you're doing it and loving it!"

Karla lives in Salem, Oregon, where she enjoys working in a beautiful studio right outside the back door of her home. She lives with her husband, Don; youngest son, William; and Lucy, the family dog. Her two older sons, Shane and Kelly, currently attend college in Oregon.

There's More Online!

- **See video demonstrations:** Go to www.creativegridsusa.com to see how-to videos for each of Karla's Creative Grids rulers.

- **Find a class near you:** Check out Karla's teaching schedule, and see more of her work, at www.saginawstreetquilts.com.

- **Discover exciting projects, new techniques, and inspiring ideas:** Visit www.martingale-pub.com to find Karla's previous books and more terrific books on quilting, sewing, and more.